Praise for *Movies That Matter*

"Tremendously useful, wonderfully provocative, and delightfully well written, *Movies That Matter* reminds us that the cinema can be a powerful way to experience God. Richard Leonard, SJ, who is uniquely qualified for the task, expertly guides readers through some of the most popular recent films and shows us how even the most unlikely movies can encourage us to pray and draw closer to the divine. This fascinating, lively, and often witty book will prove an invaluable resource to religious educators, college professors and high school teachers, pastors, parents, and anyone who watches movies—in other words, everyone."

> —**James Martin, SJ**
> author of *My Life with the Saints*

"Richard Leonard has made a brilliant contribution to the growing genre of Christian literature about film with *Movies That Matter: Reading Film through the Lens of Faith*. He takes us on a journey through fifty mostly contemporary films of various genres that mean a lot to him and shares his insights in reverent, practical, and pastoral tones. Religious educators for all grades will profit from this book because it provides new ways of seeing, for the teacher first of all. Each chapter opens by noting three "teachable moments" or themes to look for; the essay that follows combines the story with profound yet accessible commentary from the perspectives of faith and values; the chapter ends with three questions for personal or group reflection and dialogue. Best of all, this book is enriched by an introduction that makes the book "teachable" and "preachable," and offers realistic advice on such topics as the cinema community, sex, violence, ratings, and how to be a critical consumer—and a most helpful index at the end.

"*Movies That Matter: Reading Film through the Lens of Faith* is a book every person in pastoral ministry will want to use as he or she seeks to be relevant and faithful in a media world."

> —**Rose Pacatte, FSP**
> coauthor of *Lights, Camera, . . . Faith!:*
> *The Ten Commandments*

Movies That Matter

Movies That Matter

Reading Film
through the
Lens of Faith

Richard Leonard, SJ

LOYOLA PRESS.
A JESUIT MINISTRY
Chicago

LOYOLA PRESS.
A JESUIT MINISTRY

3441 N. Ashland Avenue
Chicago, Illinois 60657
(800) 621-1008
www.loyolapress.com

Except where otherwise noted, the Scripture quotations contained herein are from the New Revised Standard Version Bible: Catholic Edition, copyright © 1993 and 1989 by the Division of Christian Education of the National Council of the Churches of Christ in the U.S.A. Used by permission. All rights reserved.

Lyrics from "City of God" on p. 134
Text: Dan Schutte, b. 1947
Tune: Dan Schutte, b. 1947; acc. by Robert J. Batastinin, b. 1942 © 1981, Daniel L. Schutte and New Down Music. Published by OCP Publications.

Cover design by Adam Moroschan
Interior design by Erin VanWerden

Library of Congress Cataloging-in-Publication Data
Leonard, Richard, 1963-
  Movies that matter : reading film through the lens of faith / Richard Leonard.
    p. cm.
  Includes bibliographical references and index.
  ISBN-13: 978-0-8294-2201-6
  ISBN-10: 0-8294-2201-3
  1. Motion pictures—Moral and ethical aspects. 2. Motion pictures—Religious aspects—Christianity. I. Title.
PN1995.5.L44 2006
791.43'6823—dc22
                                                                2005037494
Printed in the United States of America
09 10 11 12 13 14 Versa 10 9 8 7 6 5 4 3 2

Contents

Introduction

The first question to be answered in a book entitled *Movies That Matter* is, to whom do these films matter? The simple answer is—they matter to me! Each of these films has illuminated my faith, challenged, entertained, and consoled me. And I am not the only one. Many others find in cinema a rich repository of images that celebrate the human spirit and put us in touch with the divine. You will have your own list. Your favorite films may appear if we publish a sequel, in classic Hollywood style: *Movies That Matter II: The Films That Got Away!* For now, I would take it as a compliment if you argue the selections in this book. That means we are starting on the same page—taking film seriously. The multiplex is the modern market for ideas and values. It is shaping us, whether we like it or not.

In these essays you will find a method for analyzing and understanding films as they explore, reinterpret, or undermine Christian theology. Some movies will be familiar; I hope these reflections will help you see them afresh. For those titles you have not seen, may these essays encourage you to explore them. I hope this book functions as a discerning guide as well as a basis for stimulating discussions.

Why should Christians take movies seriously?

When the great missionary St. Francis Xavier left Rome for the Far East, St. Ignatius of Loyola advised him: *wherever you go, learn the language.* Learning a new language is hard, especially at an advanced age, but the cultural understanding it provides amply rewards the effort. The influence of media in creating and reflecting culture means there is a new language being spoken that is well worth learning.

Given the power of media, becoming conversant with its mixed messages is an essential tool for Christian life. This involves the process of inculturation—discovering where Christ is already active within a given culture. Inculturation has traditionally been about uncovering Christian resonances in faraway places and exotic rituals. Yet the risen Christ sends us out to our media-saturated culture as well, and in it we labor with Christ to expose the signs of God's saving love already present there. We cannot speak to a culture we do not know or one we despise. And if we don't evangelize it, who else will? In St. Ignatius's terms, we have to learn its language and discover how Christ has already gone ahead of us, inculturated in some of media's values, stories, and style.

Jesus is an outstanding example of media inculturation. In Matthew 13, Jesus would not speak to the crowd without a parable. Jesus understood that our most important lessons are learned through stories—while we are laughing or crying, being confronted or consoled.

Whether we like it or not, the cinema is the place where an increasing number of people encounter a world of otherness, of ethical systems and personal and social mythologies that transcend the everyday. This encounter leads to a new consciousness of our surroundings, ideologies, and moral imperatives. As Margaret Miles rightly argues in her book *Seeing and Believing: Religion and Values in the Movies*, "The development of popular film coincided historically and geographically with the emancipation of public life from church control and patronage. 'Congregations' became 'audiences' as film created a new public sphere in which, under the guise of 'entertainment' values are formulated, circulated, resisted, and negotiated" (Miles 1996, 25).

How do we "read" a film from a Christian point of view?

Sadly, some Christians believe that unless a movie is about Jesus or the saints, unless it speaks of religion or wears its spirituality on its sleeve, it cannot be counted in the cinematic Christian canon. Some believers dismiss film altogether: "Only sex and violence sells at the cinema," or "There is nothing good at the movies anymore." These uninformed comments deny the idea that a story might be consonant with the Christian message even though it never mentions Jesus, the Bible, or the church.

To respond, let's take the top ten grossing box office films of all time.

1. Titanic (1997): $1.845 billion
2. The Lord of the Rings: The Return of the King (2003): $1.118 billion
3. Harry Potter and the Sorcerer's Stone (2001): $976.5 million

4. The Lord of the Rings: The Two Towers (2002):
$926 million

5. Star Wars: Episode I—The Phantom Menace (1999):
$924.5 million

6. Shrek 2 (2004): $918.7 million

7. Jurassic Park (1993): $914.7 million

8. Harry Potter and the Chamber of Secrets (2002):
$867.7 million

9. The Lord of the Rings: The Fellowship of the Ring (2001):
$871.1 million

10. Finding Nemo (2003): $864.4 million

(Source: Box Office Mojo)

All of these films are family entertainment. They vary in quality and some have adult themes, but none are overly sexy or violent. With *Forrest Gump, The Lion King, Star Wars: Episode II—Attack of the Clones, Star Wars: Episode VI—Return of the Jedi, Independence Day, The Sixth Sense,* and *Star Wars: Episode V—The Empire Strikes Back* making up most of the top twenty, one of the things we might stop saying is that only sex and violence sell in the cinema. If filmmakers want to do well at the box office, they should make films the whole family can watch.

The second thing we should note is the dominance of science fantasy. Six of the top ten films are set in other worlds where metaphysics is of a high order, transcendence is a given, and belief in other beings is assumed. These worlds may not be Christian, but in regard to the idea of transcendent realities that are influenced by present choices they are of a similar mind. The top ten box office films indicate a genuine thirst for the spiritual, and evidence that the younger generation does not lack the ability to imagine big stories, other worlds, and sacrificial values.

With the preponderance of films from the period 2001–2003, the above table is unfair. If, however, we adjust for inflation, then the top ten grossing box office films of all time look like this:

1. Gone with the Wind (1939): $1.26 billon
2. Star Wars (1977): $1.1 billion
3. The Sound of Music (1965): $890 million
4. ET the Extra-Terrestrial (1982): $886 million
5. The Ten Commandments (1956): $818.7 million
6. Titanic (1997): $802 million
7. Jaws (1975): $800 million
8. Doctor Zhivago (1965): $691 million
9. The Exorcist (1973): $691 million
10. Snow White and the Seven Dwarfs (1937): $681.2 million

(Source: Box Office Mojo)

With the exception of *Jaws* and *The Exorcist*, our observations about family entertainment hold firm. Across generations more publicly religious and churchgoing, science fantasy counts for less and religious-themed films such as *The Sound of Music, The Ten Commandments,* and *The Exorcist* all feature. What is consistent is the bigness of the stories, the other worlds they open up, and the sacrificial values they enshrine.

Reading a film in the light of faith starts with having the eyes to see, the ears to hear, and the heart to receive what is good and enjoyable in media culture. This task is akin to Mark 16, where the young man robed in white instructs Peter and the women to meet the risen Lord in Galilee. This invitation makes them afraid. Jerusalem was the holy city, whereas Galilee was their everyday turf. And yet it is precisely there that the risen Christ wants to meet them. Galilee is now a state of mind, a belief that God can be found where we are. Given that the cinema now sells over one billion tickets a year, I am convinced this is one of the everyday patches of turf wherein Christ is revealed.

Virtues and Values

St. Paul tells us the greatest virtues are faith, hope, and love. These are known as the theological virtues, which make us discernibly Christian. St. Thomas Aquinas added to these justice, fidelity, self-esteem, and prudence, now termed the cardinal virtues. Added to the virtues are their applications—mercy and hospitality, the Christian values. St. Thomas argued that wherever faith, hope, love, justice, fidelity, self-esteem, prudence, mercy, and hospitality are present, then named or not, Christ is present. The best of missionary dialogue has been conducted on this basis, recognizing and affirming the goodness in culture. What applies to non-Christian cultures equally applies to non-Christian elements in our own culture—at the multiplex.

We approach the task of inculturation by not being against everything. If a film presents virtues and values, and many do, then named or not, Christ is present in and through them. We should say yes to these movies and promote them. Yet we often insist that the world talk our talk and walk our walk. Jesus' great commission to go out to the world does not lead to that conclusion. Rather, Christ sends us to meet our sisters and brothers where they are, as they are. Again, Jesus is our model. The parables do not mention God. They rarely have a religious setting. Jesus takes ordinary events of daily life and draws out lessons about faith, hope, love, justice, fidelity, self-esteem, prudence, mercy, and hospitality. The cinema's parables can provide us with a venue in which to fulfill the great commission.

The Seven Deadly Sins

Our second task is not to be immediately frightened of the dark world movies often explore. We hold to faith in a world that is broken and sinful. So did Jesus, and into this same world he sends us. The Christian tradition has summed up the worst human excesses in the seven deadly sins: pride, greed, envy, anger, lust, gluttony, and sloth. Christians used to hear about these sins too much; these days we hardly mention them at all. But that doesn't mean they have gone away. Most personal, national, or international problems can usually be brought home to one or more of the seven deadly sins.

Our concern is not whether a story explores sin, but whether it is glamorized and seen as normal. By glamorized I mean made to seem not deadly at all, but life giving. Movies may seem to deny the destruction and alienation of sin and suggest it brings happiness, popularity, and success. This is a lie, and we need to say so. The second thing some films do is promote the idea that destructive behavior is normal, a reality of the human condition. Christianity holds that pride, greed, envy, anger, lust, gluttony, and sloth are not humanity's normal destiny. We are better than our worst behavior, and we can make amends, new choices, and start again. Films that present dark behavior as normal should be challenged.

Some films explore human darkness and suggest that it is glamorous and normal. In the preaching traditions of the church, people were often invited to imagine what the world would be like if God's love was absent. This tradition is immortalized in the media of past generations—stained glass, paintings, sculpture, and illuminated manuscripts. Our forebears knew that sometimes it is necessary to contemplate consequences in order to make the best choices. Parables of sinful behavior on the silver screen can be put at the service of the gospel as long as it is clear that the wages of sin is death, in one form or another.

Community and Belonging

A third signpost on the road to inculturating the multiplex is to consider trends emerging in the movies. Five trends stand out for me. The first is a longing for community, for being connected to each other. *Finding Nemo, Cast Away, Gladiator, My Big Fat Greek Wedding, American Beauty, Erin Brockovich,* and *Notting Hill* are movies in which community is central, even in its absence.

The church seeks to embody and promote the ideal of community. A worrying trend in film is how the blood family is denigrated or dismissed, faithful marriage cheapened, and the peer group established as the primary source of care in a person's life.

The building of community should not normatively come at the cost of undermining the old-fashioned family unit.

Sex

The presentation of sexuality in movies is the second trend of which we need to be aware. Pushing the sexual envelope is not a recent phenomenon. Films that broke various sexual boundaries include *Midnight Cowboy* (1969), *A Clockwork Orange* (1971), *Last Tango in Paris* (1972), *Salo, or The 120 Days of Sodom* (1976), *La Cage aux folles* (1978), *The Last Temptation of Christ* (1988), *The Cook, the Thief, His Wife, and Her Lover* (1989), *The Crying Game* (1992), *Philadelphia* (1993), *Lolita* (1997), *The Idiots* (1998), *Eyes Wide Shut* (1999), *Intimacy* (2001), *Baise-Moi* (2000), and *Nine Songs* (2004).

Christians approach sexuality as a gift to be enjoyed, nurtured, and developed. Our sexuality is not meant to bring shame and guilt. The context within which sexuality reaches fulfillment is the one in which we are assured of trust, fidelity, and care: lifelong, monogamous marriage. The worrying trend in film is that sex is treated as one of many recreational options. Casual sex reduces our bodies to a commodity traded for fun or favors, rather than as part of the celebration we share to express the sacrificial love between spouses.

In 1992 Cardinal Roger Mahony of Los Angeles outlined seven questions for Christians to consider about the portrayal of sex in media: Does the story demand it? When the characters are portrayed as engaging in sexual relations, what are they saying to each other? Is the sexual relationship being promoted as one of human dignity and trust? Is the sex primarily about pleasure, devoid of lifelong commitment? What messages is it conveying about body image and self-esteem? Does it involve coercion? How is it depicting the nature of women and men and the relationship between the two? These questions enable us to judge how film culture forms our attitudes toward our sexuality (see www.archdiocese.la/archbishop/letters/film/index.html).

Violence

The counterweight trend to sex is movie violence. Surveys in the last twenty years show that parents worry more about the effects of violence in movies than they do about sex. Again, the mid-1960s saw a turning point in regard to what audiences paid to see: *Dr Strangelove* (1964), *Bonnie and Clyde* (1967), *Easy Rider* (1969), *A Clockwork Orange* (1971), *The Godfather* (1972), *Taxi Driver* (1976), *Raging Bull* (1980), *Blue Velvet* (1986), *The Silence of the Lambs* (1991), *Hannibal* (2000), *Baise-Moi* (2000). Christians blame media violence for much that besets us, but it can be a convenient scapegoat. Many people watch violent material and never act out. Violent people may not view such material. A simple causal link has not been established. Human psychology is more complex than that.

However, authoritative studies do clearly establish the link between watching violent material and the desensitization to violence on and off the screen. In 2000, a report on media violence cited more than one thousand studies clinically showing how children exposed to media violence are significantly more likely to demonstrate aggressive attitudes and behavior. By the time a U.S. child reaches the age of eighteen it is estimated he or she will have witnessed two hundred thousand acts of violence on television, including twenty thousand murders (*Joint Statement on the Impact of Entertainment Violence on Children*, Congressional Public Health Summit, July 26, 2000).

One may also wonder why we do not focus on violent realities that directly impact our children and are rarely paid media attention. Domestic abuse is the most frequent form of violence to which our children are exposed. It is no respecter of class, religion, or ethnicity. Why is there a conspiracy of silence on this issue? Would it change if we had an equal number of women making films and television programs?

Another violence we endure in the cinema today is language. Censors rate films according to the coarseness of the language in a nod to standards of "decency." But swearing is not merely an offense against decency. It is a violent action that inflicts harm, a verbal assault as civil law now recognizes. This is further compounded by religiously violent language, as when we hear *Jesus* or *Christ* used. For us, *Jesus* and *Christ* are not simply two words in the vocabulary, but the focus of the most important relationship in our lives. Attending to the habits of our own speech is a real contribution to diminishing verbal violence as well.

Cardinal Mahony names four criteria to ponder regarding violence in film. "Is violence demanded by the story? Is it presented as a desirable way to solve problems and resolve conflict? Do we feel the pain and dehumanization it causes to the person on the receiving end, and to the person who engages in it? Do we see how it spawns more violence?"

Money and Celebrity

A fourth trend in film is the love of money and celebrity. The modern cinema adulates unbridled greed, rewards deceit, and promotes a dangerous insularity. For Christians, money is value neutral—what we do with it defines its morality. In Luke 12:48 Jesus proposes a guiding principle: "From everyone to whom much has been given, much will be required." This is not a message espoused in many movies. They promote a lifestyle overly focused on body image, sexual prowess, and getting one's way. Lifestyle in movies is more about rights than responsibilities and often sacrifices human dignity. The Christian lifestyle, St. Paul tells us in Galatians, is characterized by love, joy, peace, patience, kindness, goodness, faithfulness, gentleness, and self-control.

How should we approach movies that matter, and the ones that don't?

First, a story: One of the few people to get off the *Titanic* before it set sail was a priest. Irish Jesuit Frank Browne finished his studies in 1912, and for graduation his wealthy uncle sent him a first-class ticket for the *Titanic*'s maiden voyage as far as Cork. While on board an American family befriended him and offered to pay his fare to New York. He went to the now famous Marconi room and sent a telegram to his provincial in Dublin asking for permission to accept the offer. When the *Titanic* reached Cork, a telegram awaited Browne. It read: "GET OFF THAT SHIP.

PROVINCIAL." Browne was one of thirty-four passengers to go ashore in Ireland, and he took the last known photographs of the *Titanic* as it disappeared on the horizon. Browne carried that telegram with him until his death. He was fond of holding it aloft during lectures saying that it was "the only time when Holy Obedience saved a man's life."

We should not count it a retrospective blessing if we were granted leave to abandon our cultural ship, no matter how treacherous the way ahead. Easter people have the Spirit's wisdom to guide us and the lifeboat of hope, just in case.

Critical Consumer

Canadian Jesuit John Pugente in the *Media Literacy Resource Guide* offers a simple tool to help us become smarter media consumers. Pugente outlines the EABV model: event, attitude, behavior, and values.

Event. We may be sure about what media offers, but what do we take to the media? If we take boredom, we will "surf," watching anything to kill time. If we take loneliness, then we will go to the very next film rather than consider options thoughtfully. If we take arousal to the Internet, then guess which Web sites we end up in? What we take away from media is defined in part by what we bring to it.

Attitude. There is no such thing as a value-neutral program. What is left in or taken out, what is covered or not explored, also interprets the material. Good consumers try to understand what the media makers are communicating by being alert to the side of the story that is not told.

Behavior. Increasingly, producers of media seek to elicit behavior through entertainment. Large-scale advertising campaigns, product placement, merchandise tie-ins, goods, and services are all commodities up for grabs. Critical consumers are also aware of the intellectual property being sold in the media marketplace. These days a product or an idea rarely makes an appearance without paying to be there.

Values. Applying the values test to media means asking if the story, theme, and atmosphere of the film is consistent with faith, hope, and love. Does the film espouse joy, peace, patience, kindness, goodness, fidelity, gentleness, and self-control? It may emphasize one of these values over the others, but if it does not include any of them, then chances are the film cannot be reconciled with Christian values.

Compassionate Judgment

Modern Christians have been seduced into believing that we should not criticize or judge. We hear expressions like, "We are in no position to judge," "You can't judge them," and "They can't judge us." On this point we are quite confused. One of the seven gifts of the Holy Spirit is right judgment. It would seem odd if God gave us a gift not intended to be exercised. When we say "don't judge," what we mean is "don't condemn." There is a world of difference between these two. There is not a page in the Gospels where Jesus did not judge those around him. But we are explicitly told in John 8 that Jesus never condemned anyone. Condemnation belongs to God alone, but we need to be good judges, especially in regard to media. We need to cultivate discernment between wheat and chaff, resist pressure to conform and hype to buy. We want to develop what Jesus exercised—compassionate judgment to imagine the world from another's point of view. Armed with critical consumption and compassionate judgment we are less likely to be seduced by what is not life affirming and life sustaining.

Valuing Our Story

This final signpost may appear to have nothing to do with movies, but is in fact critical to viewing them. The best consumers of stories value their own. If we do not think our personal story is of worth or importance, then we may use movies to fill the void. If our experiences are not considered worth sharing, then we may surrender to the seemingly more glamorous, exciting, and action-packed life of the cinema. Most stories represented on the silver screen are unreal, whereas our lives are very real. The stars we grow fond of don't know us and probably don't want to. Movies matter because they entertain us, cast light on our lives, challenge and provoke us, help us grieve, reduce us to peals of laughter, open up other worlds, and expose some dark realities. But we know that the world of the cinema, and the stars and stories within it, is not our world. Our everyday story is of greater value than the tales in the movies because we are living it. Our lives matter more than anything else.

So here are films that have, in one way or another, prompted me to reflect on Christ and the Christian life. I went to Galilee and met Christ there—just as he promised.

Groundhog Day

Starring Bill Murray and Andie MacDowell. Directed by Harold Ramis.
Rated PG. 101 minutes. 1993.

Teachable moments: creation, conversion, Lent.

Phil Connors hates his life. As a madcap weatherman of a regional
television station, he longs to have a job where he is taken more
seriously. His anger is manifested by a deep cynicism. Annually,
Phil is sent to Punxsutawney, PA, to cover Groundhog Day where
"a rat," as he calls it, predicts whether winter will be long or short.
This Groundhog Day, however, the news crew is snowed in after
the festivities and forced to stay another night. Phil wakes up the
next morning to discover that it is February 2—again. And his
calendar stays put for thirty-four days, until he learns to like himself, love someone else, and look at life in a very different way.

The idea of life being rerun in some way or another has
become a popular theme in recent years. *Sliding Doors* and *Run*

Lola Run are excellent films in this genre, but *Groundhog Day* places the idea in a theological context. Everywhere in the film are references to the connection between this life and the next, and the nature of eternity. "Is this what you do in eternity . . . keep reliving your worst day?" Phil asks. That sounds more like purgatory to me.

The number thirty-four is a biblically significant sum. Three and four added together make seven, which scripturally indicates the work of creation, accomplished in seven days. This is a key to understanding Groundhog Day. In the story of creation the work of each day is an essential building block for the next, highlighting our interdependence on the created order. Likewise each day of Phil's re-creation holds another vital facet to claiming the self-esteem necessary to look at himself and say that this creation "is very good." Phil considers this connection when he muses, "I'm *a* god. I'm not *the* God—at least I don't think I am." His producer Rita assures him, "You're not a god, Phil. Take my word for it. This is twelve years of Catholic school talking."

Often we have days when we regret our behavior and wish we could do it all over again. This response is good if we learn from these feelings and change our behavior. Each day is for us a new creation. *Groundhog Day* teaches an important lesson: if we are unhappy, we should look at what we're doing and giving out, as much as what we are receiving or taking in. Both efforts create and re-create us. And we are the lump sum of the choices we are making.

Phil finds that the way to conversion is to answer hatred with love, lies with the truth, injury with pardon, sadness with joy, and to give to those who want to take from him. In the process he learns to be generous, loving, and lovable. Transformed, he can get on with the life he's always dreamed of living.

It's no accident that this re-creation parable occurs as winter turns toward spring. *Lent* means "spring," a time when we emerge from the routines of our worst habits and embrace the conversion each day can hold. Phil finds a new way to sum up his experience on Groundhog Day: "When Chekhov saw the long winter, he saw a winter bleak and dark and bereft of hope. Yet we know that winter is just another step in the cycle of life." The challenge for Christians is to prepare for tomorrow while living each day as if it were our last.

Questions

• What would you do differently today if it were your last day in this world?

• How did the choices you made yesterday influence your life today? How might they influence your life tomorrow?

• How would your life change if you saw each new day as a genuinely new opportunity?

The Mission

Starring Jeremy Irons, Robert De Niro, and Ray McAnally. Directed by Roland Joffé. Rated PG. 126 minutes. 1986.

Teachable moments: church and politics, discernment, discipleship.

When going to war, it helps to know who the enemy is, what we are fighting for, and what outcome is possible. This is clearer when the opponent is "out there." It is much more difficult when the opponent is in the head or the heart. *The Mission* is a war film, but its brilliance lies in that many of the important battles happen interiorly.

In eighteenth-century Paraguay, Spanish Jesuits left the settled towns for the "land above the falls." These journeys were unsuccessful because the people of that land were wary of the colonizers, who sought to sell them as slaves. At the end of the treacherous journey beyond the waterfall, Jesuit missionaries were martyred for their trouble. Yet armed only

with his Bible and oboe, Fr. Gabriel decides to make the journey himself. Captured by the Guarani people, he plays music
for them, and they are entranced. The mission above the falls
begins.

Some time later, Gabriel witnesses the handiwork of slave
traders led by Captain Rodrigo Mendoza. Gabriel visits him and
suggests that he should repent of his sins. Mendoza insists no
penance is great enough to cover them all. Gabriel assures him
there is: "Do you dare try it?" And so Mendoza is drafted into the
service of the mission.

The Jesuits find themselves caught between the papal envoy
and the colonizers in a fight for the rights of the native people.
The envoy brings orders to close the mission. Gabriel resists the
idea that the church must bow to political realities. He adds, "If
might is right, then love has no place in the world."

The story of the mission is based in history. In 1493 Pope
Alexander VI divided the world between the two great super-
powers of the day: Portugal and Spain. This arrangement worked
well enough until the riches of South America were discovered
and claimed by both countries. Rome was called on to settle dis-
putes between the two. Through the Treaty of Madrid in 1750
an exchange of land took place. The transition of authority was
bloody. The Guarani were defeated in 1758. The pope suppressed
the Jesuits in 1773.

In another historical intersection of church and politics, this
film came out in 1986, the year after the Vatican issued directives
against liberation theology. The most extreme liberation theolo-
gians were so concerned about the discrepancy between rich and

poor they were starting to advocate armed struggle. Archbishop Hélder Câmara did not advocate violence, but he famously said, "If I give food to the poor they call me a saint. If I ask why the poor have no food, they call me a communist."

In his Spiritual Exercises, St. Ignatius of Loyola offers a meditation on choosing whom to follow: Christ or a worldly leader. The worldly path leads to riches and honor, while Christ's way of simplicity and service leads to happiness in this life and eternal life. Choosing is not just a onetime decision, but a daily discernment. Each day we battle to know what to do, who to be, and to work out what, for better or worse, the world might become as a result of our decisions.

The real Christian mission is to make decisions, simple and complex, first by freeing ourselves and then by staying that way. Those who remain enmeshed in the world will lament, like Señor Hontar in *The Mission*: "The world is thus." To which Cardinal Altamirano rightly observes: "Thus have we made the world."

Questions

• What in your immediate world most needs the love of Jesus?

• Do you believe in personal and social conversion?

• What are some important life choices you've made that need to be reaffirmed each day?

A Man for All Seasons

Starring Paul Scofield, Orson Wells, Wendy Hiller, John Hurt, Robert Shaw, and Vanessa Redgrave. Directed by Fred Zinnemann. Rated G. 120 minutes. 1966.

Teachable moments: conscience, steadfastness.

The cinema has produced great films about matters of conscience. *A Man for All Seasons* is among the best because the screenplay is surgical in its dissection of the anatomy of an informed conscience. When the hero, Sir Thomas More, refuses to sign the fateful papers, the Duke of Norfolk cries: "Thomas, look at these names! Why can't you do as I did and come with us, for fellowship!" More replies, "And when we die, and you are sent to heaven for doing your conscience, and I am sent to hell for not doing mine, will you come with me, for fellowship?"

The history is familiar. King Henry VIII of England wants to divorce his wife, the devoutly Catholic Catherine of Aragon. The pope will not dissolve the bond, so Henry works to end the pope's authority over the church in England, which eventually becomes the Church *of* England. To do this, Henry needs the approval of the peers and parliament. The king regards his chancellor, Sir Thomas More, as a loyal friend.

But by 1530, Henry requires the English clergy take oaths of allegiance to him as "Supreme Head of the Church in England." Not long after, Thomas More resigns his post. When Henry insists that all peers sign the Act of Succession—recognizing his powers over church and state, as well as his new marriage—More refuses. In 1535 More is tried, found guilty of treason, and beheaded.

It is almost impossible to withstand the assault of people lying about us; worse still when they have the ear of people with influence or those close to us. More is betrayed by friends who gain favor by lying about what he has said. When one man perjures himself to become sheriff of Wales, More is incredulous: "Why Richard, it profits a man nothing to give his soul for the whole world . . . but for Wales?" Thomas More embodies the noblest of responses before such behavior: "Forgive your enemies and pray for those who persecute you." For More, any other option was not possible. His conscience defined him—just as ours defines us.

The lies count against him, but it is silence that seals Sir Thomas More's fate. Although he refused to sign the Act, he said nothing publicly that was treasonous. Yet like Jesus before Pilate, More's silence regarding the king's right to declare himself the

Supreme Head of the Church was used against him. Thomas Cromwell summarizes the case against More: "Let us consider now the circumstances of the prisoner's silence. . . . He calls this silence. Yet is there a man in this court—is there a man in this country!—who does not know Sir Thomas More's opinion of this title?" Sometimes the most eloquent testimony we can give to the truth is to say absolutely nothing. Who we are expresses everything that needs to be said.

Thomas More did not go looking for a martyr's death. There are moments, however, when to betray our principles and values would cause a dying with which we could not live. Death is not willingly sought, but is paid as the price for being born for higher things. Sir Thomas More ends his life with a simple eloquence: "I am commanded by the king to be brief, and since I am the king's obedient subject, brief I will be. I die His Majesty's good servant, but God's first."

Questions

• How did Thomas More's Christian faith inform his thoughts, conscience, and behavior?

• Have you ever had to let something die in order to be true to your conscience?

• What kinds of pressure does society try to exert on us to conform to norms which are incompatible with our Christian faith?

Ordinary People

Starring Mary Tyler Moore, Donald Sutherland, Judd Hirsch, and Timothy Hutton. Directed by Robert Redford. Rated R. 124 minutes. 1980.

Teachable moments: grief, acceptance, self-care.

The Jarrett family is in crisis. Last year Beth and Calvin lost their son Buck in a boating accident. Their second child, Conrad, survived the accident. Discharged from a psychiatric hospital following a suicide attempt, Conrad is not at ease. He believes his mother blames him for surviving. Conrad starts therapy, and as he inches toward recovery, his parents' marriage falls apart.

Ordinary People is dark and intense, but that's what gives the drama its power. It opens with Conrad's school choir singing, "O Lord we contemplate your peace." The words are instructive: this story is about the search for peace. Conrad externalizes the family's trauma, but all three are emotionally brittle.

The title is ironic: the Jarretts are not ordinary people. They are wealthy, educated, and socially connected. Beth Jarrett, especially, is conscious of appearances and of pretending that all problems can be dealt with discreetly. A tagline for the film runs, "Everything is in its proper place. . . . Except the past."

But grief is no respecter of class. The Jarretts *are* ordinary in their vulnerability to tragedy. Conrad wants to opt out, in suicide or by retreating into his own painful world. His father, Calvin, is practiced in negotiating the icy truce between his wife and son. And then there is Beth, who fusses over what tie Calvin should wear to Buck's funeral. She immediately scrubs the bathroom floor to get the blood off the tiles after Conrad's suicide attempt. When Conrad breaks a plate, Beth holds the pieces together and declares, "Oh, I think it can be saved." Cold and aloof, Beth might have been the villain, but Tyler Moore's performance is of such depth that we come to empathize even with her. Beth's contained anguish is glimpsed in an outburst after a friend awkwardly urges her to be happy: "Happy! Ward, you tell me the meaning of happy. But first you better make sure your kids are good and safe, that they haven't fallen off a horse, been hit by a car, or drowned in that swimming pool you're so proud of! . . . Then, you come and tell me how to be happy!"

The truth teller in *Ordinary People* is Dr. Berger, the therapist who warns us all, "A little advice about feelings, kiddo: don't expect it always to tickle." Not so long ago, expressing feelings was considered indulgent or impolite. Modern psychology has revealed the downside of repression. Feelings don't go away just because we will them to, but often reemerge in destructive ways. Repressed feelings lead to role-playing and using work, social success, recreation, drugs, and other "narcotic" behaviors to ward off pain.

This film was part of a turning point in recognizing the importance of owning darker feelings like grief, anger, and resentment. Dr. Berger asks Conrad, "What was the one wrong thing you did?" The boy answers poignantly, "I hung on. I stayed with the boat. I lived."

Self-care is a virtue in Christian tradition. A healthy exploration of feelings is an essential ingredient in that care. Christians need to be alert that self-care does not trip over into self-absorption—where the world revolves around my feelings, my needs, my wants—becoming part of the problem, not the solution.

And what's the antidote to that happening? Claiming an ordinary life, full of ordinary hopes, joys, and anxieties. Our feelings and issues are more manageable from this perspective, especially when other ordinary people share the burden.

Questions

- Do you see the problems of Conrad and the Jarrett family as problems that are common among many families today?

- How do you care for your emotional needs? What helps you make healthy emotional choices?

- What would you describe as the moments of grace in this movie?

Places in the Heart

Starring Sally Field, Danny Glover, Ed Harris, and John Malkovich. Directed by Robert Benton. Rated PG. 112 minutes. 1984.

Teachable moments: family, communion.

In 1935 in Waxahachie, Texas, Sheriff Royce Spalding leaves his lunch to confront a drunken man wielding a gun. The man, an African American, carelessly shoots the white sheriff and is promptly lynched. Edna Spalding is left with two children and an indebted farm. When the bank moves to foreclose, Edna must take in a blind lodger, Mr. Will, and Moze, an itinerant farm worker. To save the farm, they must win the bonus for the first cotton harvest. Moze coaches Edna in bargaining for the best cotton price. The success of a woman and "her uppity black man" causes resentment. Soon the Ku Klux Klan makes a visit to the Spalding place.

The film title describes the material the film explores, but it may also invoke Léon Bloy's famous line, "There are places in the heart that do not yet exist; suffering has to enter in for them to come to be."

Almost everyone in the story is "God-fearing," at least in church. But Edna's brother-in-law is an adulterer, the bank manager shows little compassion, and the cotton marketers don't mind cheating a woman. Some people only fear God on Sundays. Of course, the KKK doesn't fear God—just difference.

Moze is clearly a Deep South Moses. Moze's people too were forced into slavery. As outsiders, both men became indispensable to the local powers. Both needed others to speak for them—Aaron because Moses couldn't speak well, and Edna because white folk did not want to hear what Moze had to say. Both men knew hard, testing times, hoped in a Promised Land, but neither enjoyed the realization of their dream.

Places in the Heart can also be viewed as a meditation on the Lord's Prayer:

Our Father, who art in heaven, hallowed be thy name. In the opening scene, families of all colors enjoy Sunday lunch—keeping holy the Lord's Day. In a few hours, Royce and his assailant will be with our Father in heaven. In a few months, how God's name is made holy will change in Waxahachie.

Thy kingdom come. Thy will be done on earth, as it is in heaven. Edna reinvents herself from a submissive wife into a streetwise head of her household. On her farm, everyone discovers their best self and contributes what they can. Disability, color, and class count for nothing, as respect obliterates prejudice.

Give us this day our daily bread. Meals are an important symbol of welcome. Moze starts out eating in the shed at the back of the house, but later sits down with the family. Jesus used the meal as a metaphor for eternal life. This film makes clear that daily bread and the food of eternal life are linked.

And forgive us our trespasses, as we forgive those who trespass against us. The expanding unity on Edna's farm is in contrast to those beyond the farm's boundary who have no place for forgiveness and whose actions divide rather than unite the community.

And lead us not into temptation, but deliver us from evil. Evil visits Edna's farm and must be confronted. But evil will not have the last word, as the reading of 1 Corinthians 13:8 confirms: "Love never ends." To amplify this point, the final scene includes all who were lost in the film singing and sharing communion together. This "end-times" ending reminds us that all have a place in God's heart.

Questions

• Has there been a time of personal suffering in your life that, like Edna's, became a catalyst for transformation?

• What is the meaning of the movie's last scene for you?

• If you were in the final scene of this movie, who from your life would be there with you?

Witness

Starring Harrison Ford, Kelly McGillis, Lukas Haas, and Danny Glover.
Directed by Peter Weir.
Rated R. 112 minutes. 1985.

Teachable moments: awakening, conversion, pacifism.

After Rachel Lapp's husband dies, she and her son travel to her sister's home. It is little Samuel's first time outside the Amish community. While changing trains in Philadelphia, Samuel becomes the sole witness to a murder. Senior Detective John Book is sent to investigate. When Samuel identifies one of Book's fellow police officers as the killer, Rachel and Samuel's lives are put in danger.

Attempting to rescue this family, Book is shot, yet they manage to flee together to Lancaster County, Rachel's home. Book literally wakes up in a foreign land. Rachel's father, Eli, and her Amish suitor Daniel watch apprehensively as Book and Rachel fall in love. Meanwhile the past catches up with them, and Book must decide to which world he belongs.

Witness is an explicitly religious story. It is no accident that a man named Book, who has lived by the book, comes to a community ruled by The Book. Eli is the elderly priest in 1 Samuel who foretells Samuel's birth and directs his path. Samuel grows up to be a great judge of Israel. Daniel is placed in a lion's den, where his prayer is heard. In Genesis, Rachel becomes one of the great matriarchs of Israel.

Witness explores the peaceful agrarian world of the Amish, contrasting it with the violent and corrupt urban landscape. The Amish hold to a literal interpretation of the Bible, the centrality of family life, communal self-sufficiency, pacifism, humility in dress and behavior, simplicity of lifestyle, and a strict ordering of rituals and structures. Rejecting photography, film, and television as graven images, ironically any member of the Amish community caught watching *Witness* would be "shunned."

In this mystical quest film, we join John Book in an inward journey of self-discovery. The film was originally titled *Called Home*. The name change is significant, because as fellow travelers with Book, we witness a world where the boundaries between the real and the unreal, physical and spiritual, conscious and unconsciousness, Eden and Sodom are manifest.

Witness opens with a funeral and closes with Book's departure. In both cases, farewell is surrounded by travel. In the opening of the film, the Amish "rise up" from the earth as they head to Jacob Lapp's funeral to celebrate that his soul has been transported to heaven. At the end of *Witness*, a similar transformation has occurred in John Book. At the car, Eli Lapp tells him, "You be careful out there among them English." Book waves and drives up the hill. The entire film is about rites of passage and charts a rite of transformation: from the confidence of the Amish belief that the dead move over from this world to the next to Book's movement from near death to the possibility of living spiritually and nonviolently.

Weir flags these interests with insights from Carl Jung. For Jung, spiritual wholeness comes through healing the split between the conscious and unconscious worlds and reclaiming the shadow side of one's personality. For John Book this involves reclaiming his feminine side (Rachel) and his inner child (Samuel). It means coming to grips with a metaphysical world (the Amish community), where nonviolence is possible. It also means living closer to the earth.

Like all quests, this one comes at a cost. Book experiences the pain of intimacy, the inability to fully possess the object of his love, and the sacrifice of farewell. He returns to his world an illuminated man. We are left to think about how to achieve the same destiny.

Questions

- What have you learned from meeting and getting to know people of other religious traditions as John Book does in this film?

- What difficulties have you encountered in attempting to integrate a new awareness into your personal life?

- What unique understandings could you bring to a conversation between people of different religious backgrounds?

Hannah and Her Sisters

Starring Woody Allen, Mia Farrow, Carrie Fisher, Dianne Wiest, and Michael Caine. Written and directed by Woody Allen. Rated PG-13. 103 minutes. 1986.

Teachable moments: maturity, responsibility, self-respect.

Hannah is almost perfect: a celebrated actress, a loving wife, mother, daughter, and sister. She is also the family peacemaker. These skills are tested as her husband, Elliot, falls for her sister Lee. Lee's partner, the emotionally violent Frederick, and Hannah's hypochondriac ex-husband, Mickey, add to the mix. Meanwhile Hannah's sister Holly writes a best seller about her wildly dysfunctional family.

These days, television and the cinema commonly explore family dysfunction. But that was not always the case. *Father

Knows Best, Leave It to Beaver, and *Ozzie and Harriet* once presented an idealized portrait of the American family and how it behaved. This was a tyranny of sorts. Woody Allen took the opposite route with many of his films, which often revolve around families out of control. Allen helps us laugh at dysfunction. By contrast, many of our families don't look so bad.

For better or worse, families contribute to who we are. We may spend our lives fulfilling or reacting against the formation we originally received. Apart from criminal action or tragic neglect, most of us deal with a legacy that is almost always a mixed bag of memories and values. Most adults at some stage stop blaming their families for sins of commission and omission and take responsibility for their destinies. *Hannah and Her Sisters* shows what happens when we don't.

There is power in blaming and seduction in the quick fix. Everyone except Hannah blames someone (often Hannah) for his or her unhappiness and angst. This is the world of "if only": if only my mother had done this, if only my family had been more like that. Though our problems may have roots in the family system, adults also have choices to make in the here and now. Blame keeps the issue "out there," promotes victimhood, and robs us of personal power. Anger may immobilize us, leading us to seek some form of narcotic to dull the pain. Elliot and Lee go for sex. Holly goes for sloth. Frederick goes for booze and anger. Mickey goes for everything.

Mickey wants the quick fix. He is obsessed with his health but rejects physical exercise. He wants to be happy but can't enjoy anything. And most of all he wants to believe in something.

Along the way he turns toward, among other things, the Hare Krishnas and Catholicism. When asked, "Why Catholicism?" Mickey is vague. "Well, you know . . . first of all, because it's a very beautiful religion. It's very well structured. . . . I'm willing to do anything." His true motive is more practical: "Catholicism was for me—die now, pay later."

Like many people, Mickey confuses religion with another product to dull the pain. Religion invites us into relationships with God, each other, and the world in which we cannot hide from the pain of living. Rather, these relationships save us from ourselves, offer closure on our past, and move us into the future with hope.

Hannah just wants peace, and her way of coping is to be the family dumping ground. But peace at dignity's expense is no peace at all. She ends up isolated because she appears invincible. As Elliot puts it, "It's hard to be around someone who gives so much and needs so little in return!" Being the communal dump is no way to happiness.

As Mickey laments, "I gotta have something to believe in, otherwise life is just meaningless." Amen to that!

Questions

• How does blaming others sabotage your own personal growth?

• Does Hannah "keeping the peace" come at the cost of creating unhealthy relationships within her family?

• What happens to a person when they use religion as just another product to dull the pain of living?

Babette's Feast

Starring Stéphane Audran, Birgitte Federspiel, and Bodil Kjer. Directed by Gabriel Axel. Rated G. 102 minutes. 1987. Danish/French with English subtitles.

Teachable moments: Eucharist, hospitality.

A mysterious woman comes to a remote village occupied by strict Calvinists. The community's founder has died, and his two daughters engage the stranger, Babette, to be their cook. They have no idea what has brought Babette to their home as she assumes the role of servant. When Babette wins the lottery, she asks for permission to provide a feast in honor of what would have been the pastor's one hundredth birthday. She spends all her winnings preparing this banquet for the community.

On the night of the meal the community is anxious. They are not used to rich fare and have never tasted alcohol. They decide to consume the feast but refuse to celebrate it, offering it up as reparation for sin. At the banquet is an army general who remembers enjoying a similar feast at the hands of Paris's most celebrated chef, a woman. Babette remains unseen throughout dinner, but despite all resistance, her meal has a dramatic effect on the diners. Stories are shared, enmities resolved, and a new unity celebrated.

Like the secrecy of Jesus' identity in Mark's Gospel, Babette's story is only gradually revealed. Laboring away in hiddenness, Babette comes into power with the lottery. The sisters who rely on her expect that Babette will abandon them in her newfound wealth. Yet Babette remains faithful, having become poor and making her home among the poor. With the winnings, she executes the meal she has longed to provide for them, pouring all she has into it.

This meal is profoundly eucharistic, as the best of everything is provided for rich and poor alike. But the effect of this meal most reveals its nature. Twelve diners surround the table. Eleven of them fear this abundance as an instrument of the devil. Only the general interprets the signs and appreciates the fare placed before him. The meal's effect, however, is indiscriminate in bringing forth truth, forgiveness, and unity.

Christian symbols abound in the film: the sea, fishing boats, and nets evoke Gospel narratives of abundance, discipleship, and the church. A hymn about the new Jerusalem begins the film and remains its theme, casting the film as a commentary on the end of time.

Windows too are a prominent symbol. A neighbor watches a young soldier arriving to court one of the sisters; later, the soldier looks out another window as he reflects on the sister's decision. Babette looks out the window reflecting on the world beyond these shores; one of her regular tasks is to wash and polish the windows. Windows are a cinematic device usually denoting other worlds, but it is no accident that we call the eyes "the window to the soul." So much of this film revolves around who's lost and found—which is the journey of every soul—and the view from the window narrates the tale.

Babette is not the first female Christ figure in the cinema. Some important films with such a figure include *The Passion of Joan of Arc* (1928), *The Song of Bernadette* (1943), *The Inn of the Sixth Happiness* (1958), *The Hiding Place* (1975), *Sophie's Choice* (1982), and *The Dark Crystal* (1982). Unlike most, Babette does not give her physical life for a cause, though in many respects she has died to her old life and been reborn to this one. However we interpret Babette—as culinary artist, Christ figure, or priest— the ability of her meal to transform lives is beyond dispute.

Questions

• In what ways does the feast that Babette prepares mirror the Passover feast shared by Jesus and his disciples at the Last Supper?

• What role does hospitality play in Christian tradition and in other faith traditions?

• How are we transformed when we receive communion?

The Name
of the Rose

Starring Sean Connery, F. Murray Abraham, and Christian Slater. Directed
by Jean-Jacques Annaud. Rated R. 130 minutes. 1986.

Teachable moments: whole sexuality, death, laughter.

In the fourteenth century, at a Benedictine monastery in Italy,
monks are dying. The dead monks were young, clever, and handsome. At first the abbot suspects suicide. He calls for Franciscan
theologian William of Baskerville to investigate, and William
quickly deduces a murderer in the cloister. The bodies keep piling
up as the abbott announces the arrival of the Dominican inquisitor, Bernardo Gui.

Gui and Baskerville have unhappily crossed swords before.
Baskerville was once an inquisitor: "But in the early days, when
the Inquisition strove to guide, not to punish." William and

Bernardo set out to find the truth about the deaths. Baskerville uses logic, deduction, and analysis. Bernardo prefers instruments of torture, convinced the devil is at play. After meeting the inhabitants of this monastery—most of them mad, bad, or grotesque—I thought the dead had received a happy release.

Underlying the story is the interplay between sex and death. Sex is vital to this film because it is so noticeably absent, or, more acurately, is repressed and controlled. Only two women appear in the narrative, one of which is the Blessed Virgin Mary, adored by the monks as an example of purity and chastity. Mary never speaks, but her image is regularly invoked as she presides over the activities of the monks. Like the woman in the Gospels who anoints Jesus' feet, the other woman has no name but is referred to simply as "the girl." Like the Blessed Mother she doesn't speak. Unlike Mary, she is not chaste and presides over a monk breaking his vow of chastity. The girl pays a terrible price.

Sexuality and death are two of the powerful, irresistible forces with which human beings have to deal. We can try and ignore them, repress them, and cheat them, but they will have the last word. The more they are seen as integral to human nature, are dealt with in the open, and all are seen as a gifts in vastly differing ways, the more constructive their role can be in our personalities and spiritual lives.

When we become frightened by unseen and unknown forces in our lives, we can try to cover them up, overspiritualize them, and resort to power to get everything under control. This movement is death dealing. As Baskerville says, "The only evidence I see of the Antichrist here is everyone's desire to see him at work."

Even today there are some Christians who speak about evil so much that one wonders whether they have actually experienced the power of Christ's resurrection. Our embracing of freedom and life in Christ never minimizes evil, but places it in context and gives us courage to confront evil confidently and consistently.

In *The Name of the Rose*, humor becomes the doorway through which the devil is presumed to enter our hearts. As one character explains, "Laughter kills fear, and without fear there can be no faith." Rightly, Christianity takes itself seriously. Our forebears gave their lives for the faith we often take for granted. But sometimes we take ourselves a little too seriously, as though, indeed, God had no sense of humor. Curiously, humor is a useful ally in approaching sex and death. Neither are frivolous matters, but humor keeps us grounded in reality about our humanity in the first case, and Christ's divinity in the second.

Questions

• What might be the significance of Brother Baskerville's name?

• How would you distinguish the intentions and methods of Bernardo Gui from those of Brother Baskerville?

• What is the nature of the evil troubling the monastery in *The Name of the Rose*?

Gandhi

Starring Ben Kingsley, Candice Bergen, Edward Fox, and Martin Sheen. Directed by Richard Attenborough. Rated PG. 188 minutes. 1982.

Teachable moments: justice, nonviolence, interfaith dialogue.

"His goal was freedom for India. His strategy was peace. His weapon was his humanity." The tagline provides a summary of the life of one of the world's most extraordinary sons. Mohandas K. Gandhi was born in India in 1869. At age seventeen, he left for London where he studied law. In 1893 he moved to South Africa, but soon felt the repression of the apartheid regime and became increasingly involved in nonviolent protests against it. When Gandhi returned to India, he engaged the struggle for Indian independence from the British.

Although Gandhi never advocated violent attacks, he was jailed four times from 1922–1942. In 1930 Gandhi led a procession of fellow Indians to the sea to protest the British monopoly on the production and sale of India's salt. Until his assassination on January 30, 1948, Gandhi worked for independence and twice went on hunger strikes to protest the violence erupting during negotiations.

Gandhi advocated social change through nonviolence—a vexed issue for many Christians, the vast majority of whom are not pacifist. We allow for proportionate violence as a last resort, especially when needed to repel a greater evil. Gandhi, however, advocated strict pacifism, famously asserting: "An eye for an eye only ends up making the whole world blind." This position requires immense discipline, and also demands that we take a long view of history. We must also not mistake nonviolence as passivity. Gandhi exercised every form of civil disobedience—complete noncooperation with unjust authorities. In his view, civil disobedience became passionately active. It also requires divine patience.

Christianity upholds the right of nations and individuals to self-defense. It considers that some violent actions can render a greater good for a greater number. In this view not all acts of violence are inherently wrong. Gandhi would disagree: "They may torture my body, break my bones, even kill me, then they will have my dead body. NOT MY OBEDIENCE!"

Gandhi's other major contribution was interfaith dialogue. Although famous as a Hindu sage, he did not think of himself as belonging to any one religion. He declared, "I am a Muslim and a Hindu and a Christian and a Jew, and so are all of you." Because of the physical violence he witnessed and endured in South Africa and India, and the political violence meted out to him in England, he was understandably tough on Christians. "I would be a Christian, if it wasn't for Christians," he once said. Often Gandhi spoke in admiration of Jesus and his teachings. He considered the Beatitudes among the finest statements ever uttered, but he did not see Christians living them.

In recent years some long-standing suspicions and enmities between major faith traditions have broken down. Many now seek what unites rather than divides us. A peaceful and just world is something we can only build together. Respect and understanding between the world's religions is a good start on that road. A Hindu once despaired that he had killed a Muslim child in retaliation for the death of his own son. Gandhi counseled him: "I know a way out of Hell. Find a child, a child whose mother and father were killed, and raise him as your own. Only be sure that he is a Muslim and that you raise him as one."

The last scene of this film depicts Gandhi's funeral. The original event was one of the largest gatherings in history. Albert Einstein concluded, "Generations to come will scarce believe that such a one as this ever in flesh and blood walked upon this earth."

Questions

• What are the benefits and risks of nonviolent protest as practiced by Gandhi?

• How can interfaith dialogue help one to live her or his faith more fully?

• Are there things that people of different religious traditions can do better together than apart?

Dead Poets Society

Starring Robin Williams, Ethan Hawke, and Robert Sean Leonard.
Directed by Peter Weir. Rated PG. 128 minutes. 1989.

Teachable moments: courage, vocation, free will.

John Keating returns to teach English at his alma mater, an exclusive boys' school in Vermont. He found it stuffy there as a boy, so he sets out to change the rules. He tells his senior literature class about a group he founded as a student there, the Dead Poets Society. He urges them, "Boys, you must strive to find your own voice. Because the longer you wait to begin, the less likely you are to find it at all." His students revive the fraternity, encouraging each other to go after their dreams. Todd is shy, but wants to be a writer. Neil wants to be an actor; his parents want him to go into the military. Charlie is deeply in love with a girl in town.

The principal and staff do not appreciate Keating's methods, nor do the boys' parents. One by one the boys are set free, except for Neil. He feels trapped by the future his father has planned for him. Neil wants to perform in a play but risks his father's disapproval. Keating insists Neil tell his father about his true passion. Neil asks, "Is there an easier way?" Keating assures him there isn't. "I'm trapped!" Neil replies. Keating corrects him, "No, you're not."

Few films have placed a phrase on the lips of the world the way *carpe diem* (seize the day) entered our lexicon as a result of *Dead Poets Society*. Its poetic use comes from Horace (65–8 BC), "Even while we speak, envious time has passed: Seize the day, putting as little trust as possible in tomorrow!" The phrase originally meant that one should live fully now because we can never be sure what the gods have in store for us. This parallels Christ's promise that we should live life and live it to the full.

While *Dead Poets Society* advocates the joy of freedom, it may not give equal airplay to freedom's necessary traveling companion: responsibility. The film is unbalanced on this score, though Keating rightly warns his charges, "There is a time for daring and a time for caution, and a wise man knows which is called for." We Christians cannot act as though our own lives, desires, and futures were all that counted. In Scripture it is the whole people of God whom God comes to enliven, redeem, and save. Some might say, "If I was the only person in the world Jesus would still have lived, died, and been raised from the dead for me." Yet even this personal confession of gratitude must be viewed within the wider canvas and the bigger story. As Christians we don't resent this, but rejoice that our choices are always checked and balanced by the needs of the community. This film reveals the tragedy of trying to negotiate with the world on an all-or-nothing basis.

No matter how difficult life gets, we are one choice away from starting to live a better life. When Keating stands on his desk, he asks, "Why do I stand up here?" One student suggests, "To feel taller!" Keating replies, "I stand upon my desk to remind myself that we must constantly look at things in a different way."

As Christians we find happiness in searching for beauty and truth in concert with others. Seizing the day includes seizing each other with new ideas, great visions, enthusiasm, and a love that enables everyone to capture their dream.

Questions

• What does "seize the day" mean to you?

• How do you follow John Keating's advice to always try to see things in a different way?

• Would you describe Mr. Keating as a responsible teacher? Why or why not?

Romero

Starring Raul Julia, Richard Jordan, and Eddie Velez. Directed by John Duigan. Rated PG-13. 102 minutes. 1989.

Teachable moments: social justice, martyrdom.

A buzzword in social justice circles these days is "conscientization." When exposed to a new idea or situation, we become disposed to a new way of thinking and seeing. *Romero* is an anatomy of how one man was transformed by this process.

Appointed archbishop of San Salvador in 1977, the bookish Oscar Romero was a surprise choice. El Salvador was in upheaval with a growing public defiance of the repressive government, which considered Romero a safe appointment. At first he was, but three events conscienticized him. A Jesuit priest he admired, Fr. Rutilio Grande, was killed by the military for defending the rights of workers and peasants. The people asked Romero whether he would stand with them as Fr. Grande had done. He said yes.

The second event came the following year when three bishops condemned the popular people's movement as Marxist and therefore hostile to Christianity. Romero rejected his brother bishops' claims and called the movement simple justice. Romero was now on a collision course with leaders of both church and state.

The third event came in 1979, when the largest political gathering ever held in El Salvador was organized. The military police opened fire on the unarmed crowd. From then on Romero's defense of the poor became stronger and more international. His radio appeal was bold: "When you hear a man telling you to kill, remember God's words, 'thou shalt not kill.' No soldier is obliged to obey a law contrary to the law of God. In the name of God, in the name of our tormented people, I beseech you, I implore you; in the name of God I command you to stop the repression." In March 1980, while presiding at the Eucharist, Romero was shot to death.

Our faith is built upon the witness of martyrs. In fact, the word *martyr* means "witness." All Saints' Day, celebrated throughout the world on November 1, has its roots in the early church's Martyrs' Day. Like Jesus, Christian martyrs do not go looking for death, but are put to death because they cannot live any other way. They embody liberty of spirit, thirst for justice, and witness to truth. In doing so, they may threaten powerful people so much that they have to be silenced. Romero wanted a quiet life, away from the concerns of social inequality, a life that focused on esoteric questions of philosophy. Through a gradual conscientization he realized that the gospel calls Christians to work for the reign of Christ here on earth, not just in heaven. This reign has social and political dimensions, whereby the dignity and needs of the poor and vulnerable must be protected, nurtured, and respected. When the poor have no one to fight for them, the church must be their voice. Romero embodied what the church calls its preferential option for the poor.

The film ends as Archbishop Romero at Mass, minutes before he is shot, performs the rites for the preparation of the gifts. It was an extraordinary moment to die. In the Eucharist we don't just remember that Jesus saved us, but that his saving actions are present here and now. Romero's life was a preparation for the final gifts he would offer his own people in Christ's name: courage, sacrificial love, and his own life. And the work has only begun, for as Romero himself said: "If they kill me, I shall arise in the Salvadoran people."

Questions

- Where did Archbishop Romero find the courage to risk and ultimately lose his life standing up for the poor and powerless?

- How does the church in this country speak to the powerful as the voice of those without a voice?

- What would provide you with the courage to make a stand?

JFK

Starring Kevin Costner, Jack Lemmon, and Ed Asner. Directed by Oliver
Stone. Rated R. 189 minutes. 1991.

Teachable moments: discernment, truth.

New Orleans District Attorney Jim Garrison is unconvinced by
the findings of the Warren Commission. So he begins his own
investigations into the 1963 assassination of President John F.
Kennedy in Dallas. Eventually Garrison brings to court key
players he is convinced were involved in the assassination and
cover-up. Garrison is not afraid to entertain the most penetrat-
ing questions, as another character defines them: "Why was
Kennedy killed? Who benefited? Who has the power to cover it
up? Who?"

Director Oliver Stone knows the power of film. He has used
it to make searing statements about political causes: *Platoon,*
Born on the Fourth of July, Wall Street, Nixon, The People vs. Larry

Flynt, Salvador, and *Midnight Express.* Each of these films is critical of an element within the American establishment. *JFK* is so technically well polished, the fusing of archival and reenactment film so professional, and the tone of the film so confident, some people will think this is the definitive version of the events of that tragic November day. The problem is that it is not.

This film generated a new wave of study and debate about Kennedy's assassination. This may have been Stone's intent. Yet many who see this film will have neither the time nor the interest to follow the dissenting arguments, so they rely on this film as a historical resource. This led one commentator to retitle *JFK* as *Dancing with Facts,* given that the previous year Kevin Costner also starred in *Dances with Wolves.*

This film is helpful for Christians because in issues of public concern there are always different ways of interpreting events and various conclusions drawn from them. Though in the world and not of the world, Christians are called to be good citizens, and this means taking seriously our obligations to be informed about social and political issues. We must also hold public institutions up to scrutiny and accountability.

Journalists do this scrutinizing for a living. Democracy could not exist without them. Eighteenth-century social philosopher Edmund Burke called them "the Fourth Estate." By it he noted that the First Estate was the nobility, the Second the clergy, the Third the commons, but that "in the Reporters' Gallery yonder, there sat a Fourth Estate more important than they all." Their power is defined by the access they have to us, the voting public. We have become fond of laying a lot of blame at journalists' doors, some of it deserved. But democracies owe a debt of gratitude to the Fourth Estate for their great sacrifices in the service of the truth. This film is grounded in the Fourth Estate as lawyer Jim Garrison represents this dogged dedication to the truth.

The sensibility for us to bring to films like *JFK*, the work of investigative journalists, or intelligent conspiracy theorists, is the same one they bring to bear on the questions about which they are passionate: healthy skepticism. To form our consciences on an issue we must think of ourselves as jury members who need convincing of the facts of the case, the various sides of the debate, and the ways in which the arguments can be interpreted. We cannot simply ignore thoughtful commentators like Oliver Stone— because they just might be on to something.

Questions

- Jim Garrison appears fearless in his quest to find out the truth behind the assassination of JFK. Is he being brave or careless?

- What are some necessary steps in discerning the truth of an issue? Where can one go for help?

- What role do the media play in shaping public opinion? What is our obligation in response?

Unforgiven

Starring Clint Eastwood, Gene Hackman, Morgan Freeman, and Richard Harris. Directed by Clint Eastwood. Rated R. 131 minutes. 1992.

Teachable moments: sin, forgiveness, grace.

Bill Munny was once a paid gun, feared both for his skill and lack of pity. After he got married, he changed: gave up drinking, turned in the gun, bought a farm, raised children, and planted crops. As Bill puts it: "I'm just a fella now. I ain't no different than anyone else no more."

Then Bill's wife dies and his crops fail. He needs to feed his children. Meanwhile in Big Whiskey, Wyoming, trouble is brewing. One night a local prostitute passes sentence on the physical attributes of a cowboy customer. Incensed, he takes out a knife and slashes her face. The local sheriff fines the cowboy six horses, enraging the prostitute's collective. The women place a bounty on the cowboy's head. A bounty hunter convinces Bill to break his promise to his departed wife, take up his gun, ride with his old partner, Ned, and join him in claiming the loot. Bill knows it's not as easy as it sounds. "Hell of a thing, killin' a man. Take away all he's got and all he's ever gonna have." When the bounty hunter insists the cowboy had it coming, Bill points out, "We all got it comin', kid."

Director Clint Eastwood does for the American Western what Matthew and Luke do for Christianity. In this film, the characters are morally complex. There are no clear goodies and baddies. Bill and Ned are as good as they get, and both are relapsed ruthless contract killers. In the genealogies of Jesus, Matthew and Luke show us similar complexity. They claim as Jesus' ancestors prophets, kings, patriarchs, and heroes. They also include sinners and despots, roots most of us would prefer not to know about. A number of names in the genealogies appear nowhere else in the Bible, people whose stories are forgotten. Matthew adds five women, all of whom conceive in surprising, complex, or compromising situations. The genealogies serve as theological shorthand, keeping alive the dangerous memory of the ancestors of Jesus.

Goodness comes into being from the most extraordinary circumstances. The gift at the end does not right the wrongs of the past, but it does reveal that God refuses to be limited by history. It helps us stop whitewashing the past—religious, civil, or personal. It also helps us appreciate how much we learn along the way.

The major difference between this film and the Gospels is their titles. *Unforgiven* points to why no one emerges in the narrative as a whole person. Life has been tough on these people, unforgiving. In turn, they are merciless with others, expecting little and receiving less. By contrast, the subtitle for Luke and Matthew's Gospels could be *Forgiven*. The preeminent feature of the kingdom Jesus proclaims is forgiveness. "You have heard that it was said, 'An eye for an eye and a tooth for a tooth'. . . . But I say to you, Love your enemies and pray for those who persecute you" (Matthew 5:38, 44). Unlike *Love Story*'s motto, "Love means never having to say you're sorry," followers of Jesus are known by how we amend the wrongs we have committed and forgive those who have injured us. In being merciful to one another we pass on what we have received.

In Big Whiskey, Wyoming, people worry about just desserts. As the sheriff is dying, he laments, "I don't deserve this . . . to die like this. I was building a house." Bill sadly advises him, "Deserve's got nothin' to do with it." This could be good news, when you consider what we each may truly deserve. Thank the Lord for the dangerous memory of the mercy of God.

Questions

• How is this movie different from other Western movies you may have seen?

• In what ways does this movie take the issue of violence seriously?

• What is one important life lesson that forgiving another person has taught you?

Schindler's List

Starring Liam Neeson, Ben Kingsley, and Ralph Fiennes. Directed by Steven Spielberg. Rated R. 195 minutes. 1993.

Teachable moments: conversion, good and evil, choosing life.

Oskar Schindler was an arrogant Czech citizen who took up the Nazi cause. As Schindler smugly reflects, "My father was fond of saying you need three things in life—a good doctor, a forgiving priest, and a clever accountant. The first two, I've never had much use for." A small-time businessman with big ambitions, he seizes the opportunity to make himself rich and important during World War II. Using incarcerated Jews as slave labor, Schindler founds a munitions factory. At some point, he realizes the factory is the only thing preventing his workers from being exterminated. As the war's end approaches, Oskar determines to save his employees from the Nazi's final solution. He draws up a list of those who are, as he claims, important to the national interest. Schindler then sets about purchasing them from the Nazis. It costs him his empire. His Jewish foreman sums up the meaning of Schindler's list: "This list . . . is an absolute good. The list is life."

By the end of the war Schindler is broke and an unlikely savior. Addressing his workers a final time, he is honest about his identity: "I am a member of the Nazi Party. I'm a munitions manufacturer. I'm a profiteer of slave labor. I am . . . a criminal. At midnight, you'll be free and I'll be hunted." He then addresses the factory's SS guards, who've been ordered to dispose of the camp, and is equally frank: "Now would be the time to do it. Here they are; they're all here. This is your opportunity. Or, you could leave and return to your families as men instead of murderers."

The title of the novel upon which this film is based was *Schindler's Ark* by Thomas Keneally. It has since been retitled to coincide with the film. It's a pity. In Genesis, the ark is a sign of God's salvation. It is a metaphor for how, when faced with life and death, God enables us to choose life. In Noah's ark, only two representatives of each species are saved, but it's enough to repopulate the earth. Schindler saves only 1,100 Jews, but the film tells us that by 1993 their descendants counted more than six thousand. Schindler helped to keep these lines alive, and his ark enables the survivors to tell the story.

The saying "God writes straight with crooked lines" certainly applies to Oskar Schindler. It is clear he did not found his business empire to save lives. He was a vain and greedy man. But something changed him. In the film he comes to see the dark forces in the amoral Nazi commandant Amon Goeth. It is easy to portray Goeth and the Nazis as evil, mad, or satanic. But it's a mistake. It lets them, and us, off the hook too easily. Immorality doesn't seize people in a moment. We slowly convert to it, won over to its inhumanity. This is true of Nazism, and the malevolence in us too.

Schindler's conversion is not only about what he rejects. It is also about what he embraces. In the film his relationship with his foreman Itzhak Stern is pivotal. Stern is the moral compass of the film, assuaging Schindler's greed and appealing to his humanity. As with goodness in our own lives, once Oskar embarks on generosity he finds it an intoxicating experience. He also finds it incriminates his past. Stern assures his employer, "There will be generations because of what you did." Schindler insists, "I didn't do enough!" Stern has the last word, for Schindler and for us: "Anyone who saves one life saves the world."

Questions

• Could Oskar Schindler have done more? How? What?

• What are the challenges we face today in promoting a culture of life?

• What are the dark forces at work in our world that are in need of the light of Christ?

Shadowlands

Starring Anthony Hopkins and Debra Winger. Directed by Richard Attenborough. Rated PG. 131 minutes. 1993.

Teachable moments: prayer, faith, reconciling loss.

C. S. Lewis is best known for his Narnia series. And yet Jack, as he was called, was also a literary critic, poet, and scholar at Oxford University. In 1950 he received a visit from Mrs. Joy Gresham, an admirer from the United States. They were almost opposite personalities: Joy a gregarious divorcée and mother, Jack a shy confirmed bachelor. Joy questioned religious belief; Jack was a devout Anglican. Against the odds, affection developed between them and, in time, they married so that Joy could legally remain in England. What started as a secret marriage of convenience became much more when Joy contracted cancer. Jack discovered his love for her and his doubts in God.

Shadowlands asks all the right questions about what it is we do when we pray to God, what outcome we expect, and whether prayer changes God, or us, or both. Christians hold that God is unchanging. Sometimes, however, we pray as though God can and will change on command—our command. It's hard to reconcile a poor result in these prayers with a loving God. This is the bind C. S. Lewis gets into. When Joy becomes ill he wants a miracle, and her failure to be healed makes him angry toward God.

Jack was once an atheist who came to faith through pain—the pain of feeling aimless, unsure of life and its purpose. "I don't think God is particularly interested in keeping us happy. . . . Pain is a tool," he muses. It is true that God is not particularly interested in keeping us happy if happiness means smiling all the time. Life is too complex for that. But I think God is utterly committed to our happiness in the sense of living life to the full: joyful, content, and purposeful. Such happiness anticipates the fullness of joy we will have at the eternal banquet.

In our world we only know joy in contrast to our suffering. C. S. Lewis reflects, "The pain now is part of the happiness then." Joy agrees, "That's the deal." This doesn't mean we go looking for pain, but when it comes we accept it as part of the web of life enabling us to know and value happiness all the more. As Queen Elizabeth II said after September 11, 2001, "the degree to which we grieve is the degree to which we have loved." It's what the Taoists call the yin and yang.

By the end of the film, Jack's prayers are answered, though not in terms of the commands he has issued to God. After

Joy's death, Jack discovers that he has gained the capacity to love. Jack also lets go of an aloof deity and enters into relationship with a divine companion. "Even though I walk through the darkest valley, I fear no evil; for you are with me" (Psalm 23:4).

Shadowlands demonstrates that the real power of prayer is in stripping off our masks. We need not pretend, because God knows who we are. Jack goes from performing for God to encountering him. Jack once allowed a predictable God into his predictable life because he took few risks. Lewis's life left little room for surprise. When he meets his shadow, all the old certainties are shaken up. Jack risks believing in a loving God in an unpredictable world. This God heard his deepest prayers, the ones even this most expressive man could not express—and answered them.

Questions

- C. S. Lewis says in the movie, "The pain now is part of the happiness then." Joy Gresham agrees and says, "That's the deal." What does this mean to you?

- What did Joy Gresham teach C. S. Lewis about love?

- How can a crisis of faith become an opportunity for deepening our spiritual life?

Philadelphia

Starring Tom Hanks, Denzel Washington, Joanne Woodward, and Jason Robards. Directed by Jonathan Demme. Rated PG-13. 125 minutes. 1993.

Teachable moments: prejudice, sexuality, justice.

Andrew Beckett is a talented lawyer. He is also homosexual. Working at a prestigious conservative firm, he cannot declare his sexuality and joins in the homophobic banter of colleagues. Meanwhile he maintains a promiscuous lifestyle and contracts AIDS. As his appearance betrays his condition, his employer, Mr. Wheeler, "lets him go."

Andrew sues his former law firm, Wyatt Wheeler, for wrongful dismissal, but finding a lawyer to represent him is not easy. Andrew engages the services of Joe Miller, an insignificant African American attorney almost as homophobic as Mr. Wheeler. Andrew frames his argument on the grounds of prejudice, and Joe, no stranger to prejudice, takes the case. They prepare for the courtroom showdown with Wyatt

Wheeler as David versus Goliath. Joe appeals to the spirit of Philadelphia, where the Declaration of Independence had its birth: "I don't recall that glorious document saying anything about all straight men are created equal. I believe it says all men are created equal."

Homosexuality is a vexed issue for many Christians. Arguing from selected biblical texts or a traditional understanding of the complexities of nature, nurture, genetics, and biology, many maintain a hard line against the homosexual "lifestyle." Yet there is no one gay lifestyle to condemn. As in the heterosexual community, people express same-sex attraction in ways ranging from lifelong commitment to one partner, to celibacy, to promiscuous behavior. Christians who disapprove of homosexuality rarely make moral distinctions between these expressions as they do for heterosexuals. But the distinctions matter in both cases. Gay Christians need to hear that there is a moral aspect to the type of relationship choices they make. In *Philadelphia* Andrew Beckett makes appalling, furtive choices in regard to his orientation and pays a high price for them.

In the David and Goliath story we often miss an important detail. In 1 Samuel 17, Saul dresses David for battle in chain mail and a helmet. But David cannot walk, so he strips off his armor and confronts Goliath without protection. Goliath cannot imagine this vulnerable person overpowering him. David knows, however, that good aim is more powerful than size. The aim of Christians must be that of Christ. Following Jesus' lead, many Christians do not believe that sin leads to disease, but focus on alleviating suffering. Christian communities nurse people with AIDS in our hospitals, sit with the dying in hospice, devote funding toward research, and bury the dead with dignity. Because every human being has innate worth, discrimination against anyone is immoral.

Christians profess "a preferential option for the poor," fighting for the oppressed and marginalized. Regarding the rights and dignity of homosexual people, however, Christians have often been the oppressors. If our response to the sexual outsiders in our midst is to say "stop being who you say you are," then how do we "opt" for them in their marginalization?

Philadelphia recommends how to end discrimination: getting free from fear. All prejudice is born of fear. If we don't know enough good people of a different color, race, religion, or sexual orientation, then we cannot see the world from their perspective. Initially, Joe Miller does not want to defend Andrew Beckett, not only because of the Goliath he is up against, but also because Joe does not like gay people. The most telling battle in the film occurs not in the courtroom but in Joe's head and heart as he befriends Andrew. If we want to opt for the poor, we must count them as friends.

Questions

- What prejudices do we as individuals, families, congregations, and society need to be liberated from?

- Why does Joe Miller not want to represent Andrew Beckett when they first meet? What changes for Joe Miller?

- How is discrimination against another an immoral act?

Three Colors Trilogy

Written and directed by Krzysztof Kieslowski.

Blue

Starring Juliette Binoche and Benoît Régent. Rated R. 100 minutes. 1993. French with English subtitles.

White

Starring Julie Delpy and Zbigniew Zamachowski. Rated R. 91 minutes. 1994. French with English subtitles.

Red

Starring Iréne Jacob and Jean-Louis Trintignant. Rated R. 99 minutes. 1994. French with English subtitles.

Teachable moments: Trinity, theological virtues, the Way.

A classic trilogy is one story told in three parts. *Blue, White*, and *Red* do not tell one story. Yet these stories share a message about European society and magnify aspects of modern moral malaise. In *Blue*, we meet Julie, the wife of a renowned composer commissioned to write the "Music of the Unification of Europe." The score is nearly completed when the composer and their daughter suffer a fatal accident. Bereft, Julie rejects her old life and assumes another identity. Soon she learns her husband had a lover who carries his child. Evidence also mounts that Julie ghostwrote her husband's work. Will she complete the final score?

In *White*, Polish hairdresser Karol is married to Dominique, a beautiful Parisian. The marriage is not going well. Karol appears impotent; Dominique divorces him and then frames him for arson. Fleeing, Karol inadvertently stumbles into the underworld. He gains lucratively and is soon in over his head. Staging his death gets the underworld off his back, but after the funeral Karol meets Dominique, the sole heir to his new fortune. They finally make love. When Karol vanishes, Dominique is arrested for his murder.

In *Red*, Valentine is a model in Geneva in a tempestuous relationship with her boyfriend. She discovers her neighbor is spying on her: filming her movements and eavesdropping. Valentine is drawn into his claustrophobic world in a bid to find out if her boyfriend is faithful and whether she can rescue her troubled brother. Valentine feels at a loss to help. Her neighbor advises: "You can. Be."

Blue, White, and *Red*—the colors of the French flag—symbolize liberty, equality, and fraternity. For Christians, trilogies also suggest the Trinity, Christ—the Way, the Truth, and the Life—and the theological virtues: faith, hope, and love. *Blue* centers on the truth about Julie's husband's double life and whether Julie herself is the true composer. Her marriage is a microcosm of the European union: doomed if based on deception. Julie finds liberty in facing the truth. Swimming provides the metaphor for rebirth. Within womblike waters Julie wrestles with the truth, each time emerging a little more alive.

White focuses on equality. Karol possesses Dominique as a glamorous trophy; he does not know who he is apart from her. Unequal relationships polarize marriages, societies, and nations. Fraternity accords respect. Paternalism begets social impotence, deceit, revenge, and loss of self. Karol symbolizes a Europe in which larger nations dominate and smaller ones sacrifice their identities.

Light illuminates *Red*, from a fire's glow to the blazing sun. Valentine wants out of modeling and her relationship. Her neighbor wants out of a voyeurism in which he knows others' secrets but cannot be known and loved by them. Valentine cedes control, while the neighbor is too controlling. A unified Europe based on suspicion and manipulation is a house built on sand. The only way forward is to walk into the light. Just as the colors blue, red, and white form the one flag, so equality, liberty, and fraternity form human society, and the way, the truth, and the life we are meant to enjoy.

Questions

- How does facing the truth about ourselves, our church, our society ultimately set us free? Is there a price to be paid for this freedom?

- What questions do these three movies raise regarding the unification of Europe and the implications of this unification?

The Shawshank Redemption

Starring Tim Robbins, Morgan Freeman, and Bob Gunton. Directed by Frank Darabont. Rated R. 142 minutes. 1994.

Teachable moments: redemption, hope, freedom.

In 1947, justice could be tough—and wrong. That year Andy Dufresne's wife had an affair. After the faithless couple are shot dead, Andy is convicted of the crime and sentenced to life in prison at Shawshank Penitentiary, run by the God-fearing Warden Norton. At first the banker is treated cruelly by the guards and other inmates.

In time he is befriended by a fellow lifer, Red, the great "fixer" of the jail. Red believes Andy is innocent. After gaining Norton's trust, Andy sets to work managing a forced labor scheme and makes the warden's fortune. In 1966 Norton discovers that Andy is actually innocent of murder. The warden has the informant killed to keep Andy in jail and protect his income stream. Andy plots his escape, telling Red that if he ever gets probation he can meet him on the beach in Mexico.

Many see Andy as a Christ figure: an innocent man wrongly convicted who nonetheless sets others free. Even when the truth lets him down, Andy believes in hope and beauty. Red finds this troubling: "Let me tell you something my friend. Hope is a dangerous thing. Hope can drive a man insane." In a final note, Andy replies: "Remember, Red, hope is a good thing, maybe the best of things. And no good thing ever dies." Andy is hardly pure: he helps Norton siphon off money for sixteen years and is an accessory to crime. As much as we like Andy, ends rarely justify means.

Some Christians compare the reunion on the beach to John 21, where the risen Christ meets his disciples. There, Red finds the hope that has eluded him: "I hope to see my friend and shake his hand. I hope the Pacific is as blue as it has been in my dreams. I hope." Red knows where to find Andy because he prepared the place and showed the way. Old promises have now been kept. The reunion celebrates the love they hold for each other, hard won in the crucible of their sufferings.

The word *redemption* literally means "buying back." In the ancient world there were two types of slaves—those born or forced into slavery, and others who paid off a debt or crime by becoming enslaved. The second type could be freed if someone paid the debt. They would then be the slave of the purchaser or freed completely. Christian theology adopts the metaphor to describe how we, enslaved by destructive behavior, are liberated by Christ, who subjected himself to a sinful world, its violence and death, to set us free. Claimed by Christ, we are no longer slaves but friends.

The film engagingly narrates Christian theology: an innocent man enters the tragedy of human existence and is locked into its destructive behavior, from which no one had ever escaped. Through his example, we learn that beauty and truth are possible. He gives us hope for a new and better life. And when he makes his break, we learn we can be free as well, in our own way, in our own time. We have only to learn to live as liberated people. Red tells us what that's like: "I think it's the excitement only a free man can feel, a free man at the start of a long journey whose conclusion is uncertain. I hope I can make it across the border."

Questions

• How is the power of hope able to sustain Andy during his difficult times?

• How does belief in redemption influence our understanding of freedom?

• How does Red ultimately help Andy, and Andy help Red?

Dead Man Walking

Starring Susan Sarandon and Sean Penn. Directed by Tim Robbins. Rated R. 122 minutes. 1995.

Teachable moments: crime and punishment, forgiveness, social justice.

In rural Louisiana, Matthew Poncelet is found guilty of rape and murder. He is condemned to death and moved to death row. While exhausting all avenues for appeal, he gains the support of a Catholic nun, who accompanies him to his death by lethal injection. *Dead Man Walking* is based on the true story of Sr. Helen Prejean. She had no experience in prison chaplaincy. Yet she supported a man facing death and helped him to face himself. The heart of the matter is plain to her: "I just don't see the sense of killing people to say that killing people's wrong."

Dead Man Walking is a study in empathy as Sr. Helen reaches out to both the perpetrator and the families of the victims.

Sr. Helen never pretends Matthew is innocent; rather, she insists he take responsibility for his crimes. Her visits to the homes of the victims are harrowing, as the bereaved attack her relationship to "that animal." For Christians no one is an animal, a monster, because that lets us off the hook in regard to evil. We want to distance ourselves: "They are not us." But they are. To dismiss human beings as animals betrays our own humanity. When Sr. Helen asks Matthew for respect, he sneers, "Why? 'Cause you're a nun?" She replies, "Because I'm a person." Good and evil are in every human heart. Some give themselves over to the most destructive elements with dire consequences for all.

Acknowledging the humanity of those who sin does not excuse what they've done. But it does recognize our obligation to even our most aberrant members. Maybe this was what Jesus meant by teaching us to forgive our enemies. Once we recognize humanity in the worst of our human family, then we relinquish the license to do with them what we want. Matthew's last words are poignantly true: "I just wanna say I think killin' is wrong, no matter who does it, whether it's me or y'all or your government." Can we allow a murderer the moral high ground?

The church has an uneasy relationship with capital punishment. Once, in God's name, we presided over capital punishment ourselves. The section on capital punishment in the *Catechism of the Catholic Church* was revised not long after it was published. First it claimed the state was categorically wrong to kill its citizens. The revised text allows for extraordinary situations that warrant such a measure. We betray our uncertainty.

What we do know is that as soon as we kill someone, anyone, we lose hope of growth, conversion, and love in them. In execution we say, effectively, "You are beyond God's redemption and our ability to forgive." Both statements are untrue; or at least I hope they are. Revenge looks satisfying, yet those who exact it do not seem to have much peace. It is a false good that reduces us to the aberrant level of the person we kill.

Matthew faces the enormity of his crime by opening himself up to unconditional love—the scariest thing he ever did, and the most worthy. He glimpsed what it was like to be a full human being in the person of Helen Prejean. In this sense, *Dead Man Walking* is the best film about Christian *ministry* I know. Sr. Helen opts for the poor, and in the name of Christ becomes a murderer's confessor, advocate, and companion. Sometimes we ask the question, "What would Jesus do?" This film provides an answer.

Questions

• What personal demons does Sr. Helen have to face in herself?

• What are the ramifications of capital punishment for the Christian community?

• Why can reaching out to another as a human being be such a risky thing?

Life Is Beautiful

Starring Roberto Benigni, Nicoletta Braschi, and Giorgio Cantarini.
Directed by Roberto Benigni. Rated PG-13. 116 minutes. 1997.

Teachable moments: courage, sacrificial love.

Jewish bookkeeper Guido marries schoolteacher Dora and they
have a wonderful life together. In time they also have a son,
Giosué. When the Nazis occupy Italy, ominous signs appear
in the community: "No Jews or Dogs Allowed." Perplexed, little Giosué asks his father, "Why doesn't our shop have a 'Not
Allowed' sign?" Desiring to shield his son from the hate campaign, Guido makes light of it: "Well, tomorrow, we'll put one
up. We won't let in anything we don't like. What don't you like?"
Giosué admits he doesn't like spiders. Guido replies, "Good. I
don't like vampires. Tomorrow, we'll get a sign: 'No Spiders or
Vampires Allowed.'" Soon the Jews are rounded up and sent to

concentration camps, Guido and Giosué among them. Protecting his son from the truth just got harder.

Guido determines to hide Giosué from the Nazis and also from the horror of their environment. He convinces the five-year-old that the entire situation is an elaborate game. First prize for winning is a tank. Guido sets the rules of this incongruous game: "You can lose all your points for any one of three things. One: if you cry. Two: if you ask to see your mother. Three: if you're hungry and ask for a snack! Forget it!" Giosué buys the ruse and does as Guido tells him to gain points in the "competition."

In the end, Guido makes the ultimate sacrifice so that Giosué might live and be reunited with his mother. Carrying his son through the camp, Guido murmurs, "Dream sweet dreams. Maybe we are both dreaming."

Some Jewish and Gentile critics attacked the film for making light of the Jewish holocaust, arguing that Benigni trivialized the suffering and death of millions of people. The film does make us uncomfortable. For example, when Giosué and Guido arrive at the camp, Guido's brother is taken to the gas chambers. Giosué wonders where his uncle is going. Guido covers smoothly, "Uh . . . oh, he's playing on a different team. Goodbye, Uncle!" The evil of World War II was so atrocious that finding humor within it is very risky business.

Benigni responded to his critics by calling the film a fable about the lengths to which parents will go to protect their children from the destruction of their spirits. Indeed, *Life Is Beautiful* can be read as a satire on Nazism, much like Charlie Chaplin's *The Great Dictator* (1940). More recently, Mel Brooks's

1968 and 2005 films *The Producers* are even more satirical takes on Nazism and the plight of the Jews.

Giosué's final words in the film underscore that this story is meant to be a fable about parental love: "This is the sacrifice my father made for me." The word *fable* comes from the Latin word *fabula* meaning "talk," or "narrative." Traditionally, fables are exaggerated stories with a moral message. They can involve mythical elements, like talking animals in Aesop's fables, and be set in more modern forms, such as the works of Beatrix Potter, George Orwell, and A. A. Milne. Fables can also be stories in which hyperbole makes the details secondary to the message, as is the case with *Life Is Beautiful*.

The film reveals the depth and breadth of sacrificial love, mirroring Christ's love for us. Guido doesn't laugh at war, but uses his comic gift as a way of being kind to his son. To cloak a child from the knowledge of how dreadful human beings can be, to preserve a child's belief in humanity, is a profound answer to unspeakable evil.

Questions

- What are the pros and cons of shielding another person from evil?

- How do Guido's actions depict the power of sacrificial love?

- What is the Christian response to evil?

The Godfather; The Godfather Part II

Directed by Francis Ford Coppola.

The Godfather
Starring Marlon Brando, Al Pacino, James Caan, and Robert Duvall.
Rated R. 175 minutes. 1972.

The Godfather Part II
Starring Al Pacino, Robert Duvall, Robert De Niro, and Diane Keaton.
Rated R. 200 minutes. 1974.

Teachable moments: sin, grace, choice.

Vito Corleone is the boss of a crime family. Father to Sonny, Fredo, and Michael, surrogate father to Tom Hagen, he is also godfather to a nursery of "children" whom he uses to crown his ambitions. The nature of business for mob families is changing. Narcotics are the new thing. Vito Corleone is against drugs, but when a drug baron approaches him for protection, Vito has to take a position. He rejects the offer and is gunned down. Vito survives, but the hit makes his son Michael, a "civilian" in relation to the family business, hell-bent on revenge. A turf war ensues. Vito's eldest son, Sonny, is killed. The lot falls to Michael. A dynasty is born.

The Godfather Part II shows Don Michael in charge of the "family." Now a major player in the drug trade and Las Vegas casinos, Michael reflects on his family's roots. His father, Vito, was a poor boy who migrated from Sicily in hopes of a better life. He was soon welcomed into one of New York's crime gangs. Working for the Mafia, he became skilled at murder and controlling interests in illicit alcohol and gambling.

Now Michael must shore up the family's fortunes against new interlopers. He is threatened by an internal revolt. Don Michael wants to bequeath a worthy empire to his son Vito. Worthy, for the Corleones, is an ambiguous term.

In the New Testament, Jesus asks, "What does it profit them if they gain the whole world, but lose or forfeit themselves?" (Luke 9:25). These films demonstrate the implications of what is lost. For money, greed, and power, the Corleone family loses its soul. They preach about family and the role of honor; they partake in sacraments and invoke the saints, but without noticeable effect in their murderous lives. They gain the world and lose their humanity. Within their destructive world, people are problems to be bought, owned, used, or destroyed. And for what end?

Exploring dark themes in film is useful for Christians. We cannot be immune from the reality of evil. Our evaluation of cinematic evil rests on whether it is presented as glamorous and normal. Though the wages of sin in these films is clearly death for all sides, the destruction is simply "business." Within the Christian tradition, anger and greed are deadly sins for a reason. Revenge, parading as respect, drives the Corleones. They talk about family, loyalty, and honor, but this only confirms a misplaced sense of identity.

These films may suggest that there is nothing we can do about evil, since it's a constitutive part of the human condition. Though original sin bequeaths the propensity to be destructive, we also hold that through original grace we were made in the likeness of God. Even when "we were lost and could not find our way to God," Christ comes to save us from ourselves. The human condition is essentially good. We are always better than our worst actions. Evil is not normal.

The Corleones make violence a family career. Each generation is inducted into its charms and offered its empty promises. Kay Corleone sees abortion as the only way to put a stop to the hereditary drive toward evil. If the family baptisms were taken with more gravity, perhaps some genuine amazing grace might have resulted.

Questions

• What are the destructive forces at work in our society, families, and church that blind us to what it means to be human?

• Do you believe that most human beings are essentially good?

• What impact do Michael's choices have on the people he loves and those closest to him?

Men with Guns

Starring Federico Luppi, Damián Delgado, Dan Rivera González, and Damián Alcázar. Written and directed by John Sayles. Rated R. 127 minutes. 1997. Spanish with English subtitles.

Teachable moments: conscience, repentance, Lent.

Humberto Fuentes, a successful doctor in Guatemala City, hears disturbing reports concerning five doctors he has personally trained who went to work with the indigenous people in the mountains. Fuentes decides to search for his protégés. Almost at once he encounters the legacy of men with guns. Fuentes asks a blind woman, "Why did the men kill the people?" She replies simply, "Because they had guns, and we didn't."

Fuentes embarks on a journey in more ways than one. He travels where he has not been and sees things he had refused to believe could happen in his country. Exploitation and state-sanctioned violence shock him. What he learns about himself shocks him even more. When Fuentes discovers that the army has killed his protégés, he finds the old moorings of his life useless.

Without leaving his country, Fuentes travels to a new world where money, expertise, and social class count for nothing. When he sees the price the poor have paid, he says, "Innocence is a sin. . . . How much did I not know because I was lied to? And how much did I not know because I had a comfortable life and really didn't want to know?"

Christians observe a ritual moment when they acknowledge sins of omission and commission, "what I have done and what I have failed to do." We are usually good at being sorry for things we have actually done wrong. Repenting sins of omission can be more difficult. *Men with Guns* concerns itself primarily with such sins. Humberto stands in for all of us in the so-called First World. He is a good man, having devoted his life to health care, though his practice was restricted to private clinics. The problem with Fuentes is not goodness, but his lack of concern about anything beyond his privileged world.

Fuentes must go up into the mountains to see for himself. In the Bible, mountains are places of revelation. In the mountains, Fuentes comes to see the reality of the poor and also confronts himself. Self-discovery is a painful process, transforming us from tourists to travelers on a journey with fellow travelers. John Sayles gives Fuentes an orphaned boy, a "bad priest," and an army deserter as companions to guide him through the dense terrain of the mountains and the unknown terrain of his newly formed conscience.

St. John of the Cross wrote eloquently about this difficult journey. In *The Dark Night of the Soul*, John reflected on his own experiences of feeling God's absence, facing sinfulness, and purging himself of the things that held him back from love. Although the dark journey felt overwhelming, the experience changed John's life, the nature of his prayer, and his spiritual goals. He was less afraid of the unknown. In *Men with Guns*, Dr. Fuentes endures a dark night of the soul and must suffer the purge.

Hospitality is a great Christian virtue. We often reduce it to welcoming visitors, or even strangers, but it is more than that. Hospitality also applies to what we know and want to know about other realities. If we choose to live in ignorance in order to remain undisturbed, then we sin against hospitality. Fuentes despairs when he realizes the extent of his willful ignorance. Though the climb to true sight may be exhausting, we might welcome the journey through the dark night of the soul. For there God too may be found.

Questions

- How did Dr. Fuentes's journey become a journey of personal transformation?

- What are some lessons that people in the First World can learn from their neighbors in developing countries?

- What are the consequences of willful ignorance? For oneself? For others?

The Apostle

Starring Robert Duvall, Farrah Fawcett, and Billy Bob Thornton. Written and directed by Robert Duvall. Rated PG-13. 134 minutes. 1997.

Teachable moments: pride, conversion, evangelism.

Sonny Dewey pastors a flourishing church in Texas. He boasts, "I'm a genuine, Holy Ghost, Jesus-filled preachin' machine!" He is also a drinker and an adulterer. When his wife has an affair, Sonny bashes his rival into a coma and skips town. Arriving in Louisiana, he resolves to re-create himself. Now styled as "The Apostle E.F.," he becomes a radio preacher and reopens the local Gospel Hall. The Apostle's fame spreads far and wide, even back to Texas. Before long the police pay him a fateful visit.

In recent films, clerics are rarely presented in a positive light—and with some cause. From Jim Bakker to the Catholic child-abuse scandals, it's been open season for dark portrayals of ministry. *Going My Way* and *The Bells of St Mary's* look far too innocent now. They have been replaced by *Leap of Faith, Bad Education*, and *The Crime of Father Amaro*, to name a few.

The Apostle is another fraudulent minister—a criminal deluded by his own charisma. In Texas, he preaches a strict message while being domestically violent and a womanizer. On the road, he lies religiously to avoid capture. In Louisiana, he convinces himself that his escape is a sign of God's favor. It's no accident that the first deadly sin is pride.

Reading success as the sign of God's blessing is always problematic. While the Apostle does renovate a church and gather large and satisfied crowds while the money rolls in, God's blessing is not guaranteed. Good times may feel blessed. But what about Jesus, who died deserted by his closest disciples with little to show for his public ministry? What about the Christian martyrs? Were they cursed by God? Jesus' Beatitudes, or blessings, reveal that we are blessed by God if we find ourselves poor, in grief, campaigning for justice, being gentle, making peace, and being persecuted. The Beatitudes are a corrective to those who espouse the prosperity gospel.

Although set in 1939, *The Apostle* has resonance today. Fundamentalist Christianity fights well above its numerical weight in various parts of the world. In a free society, all are perfectly entitled to exert their influence, but poor theology remains so, no matter how forcefully it is given out. While holding a baby aloft, the much reborn Sonny says, "I don't have enough love to drive a nail in this little hand. But God did this to his only son, Jesus." The Apostle E.F. implies that the sufferings of his congregation are likewise inflicted by God. This appalling theology leads to social impotence as every catastrophe is viewed as a test to be endured rather than actively healed.

We can grow through suffering and emerge from testing times richer for them. But the origin of these events should not be assumed to be the active will of God. God did not send Jesus "to die." Jesus came "to live," to show us how to live. Jesus died because of the way he transparently, lovingly, compassionately, justly, and forgivingly lived.

Unlike the Apostle E.F.'s "gospel," God's will is found in facing up to the consequence of our actions. For Sonny, the possibility of authentic new life comes when he is arrested and must face up to his choices. Christian conversion does not obliterate our past; it places it in context. Only when we own what we have done and failed to do, can we create space for the gospel to take root in us.

Questions

• Does Sonny face the consequences of his actions?

• How can we discern God's will in our lives?

• Is living the Beatitudes a countercultural lifestyle?

The Truman Show

Starring Jim Carrey, Ed Harris, and Laura Linney. Directed by Peter Weir. Rated PG. 103 minutes. 1998.

Teachable moments: truth, free will, image of God.

Ultimate celebrities have one name: Madonna, Prince, Sting, Bono, and Cher. *The Truman Show* creator is the one-name phenomenon Christof. He fabricates an artificial town in which a man will be born, live, and die. Christof has a broadcast dedicated to Truman twenty-four hours a day. The only way to keep this show on the air is to keep Truman from guessing that his life is a fake and that everyone he knows is colluding to manipulate him. Truman gets restless, however, after meeting Sylvia, who tries to tell him he is living an illusion.

Truman dreams of overcoming his lifelong fear of water, induced early to keep him from wandering. He wants to see what lies beyond the horizon, he wants to go to Fiji. Against all odds, Truman makes a bid for freedom and goes missing. Everyone in the control room of his world is nervous while Truman, on the air as ever, has to choose what to do for the first time.

The Truman Show was ahead of its time. Thousands of hours of so-called reality shows later, it looks prophetic. We now know what producers, networks, actors, and fellow citizens will do for money and celebrity. Tragically for us, *The Truman Show* alerts Christians to a worrying trend in television.

In his Spiritual Exercises, St. Ignatius of Loyola names pride, riches, and greed the most seductive and destructive of temptations. So much unhappiness can be traced to this unholy trinity. *The Truman Show,* and the reality television it prematurely satirized, fails the most basic Christian test of respecting human dignity. We owe respect even to those who do not claim it for themselves. *The Truman Show* challenges us not to join those who think that just watching this stuff doesn't hurt anyone. If enough of us changed our viewing habits, these shows would be off the air overnight.

The Truman Show intentionally challenges common misperceptions of God. Many view God as presiding over the world with a generally benevolent intent, directing and intervening in the created order. In this schema, God also causes famines, disasters, tsunamis, and illnesses. This image of God can seem capricious and, like the character of Christof, hard to trust or to love. When Christof identifies himself as Truman's creator— or at least the creator of his show—Truman rightly asks, "Then who am I?"

We do not believe that God created us as playthings, brought into being for God's amusement. We do not hold that God sends episodes of pain, illness, and disease as punishment for our sins. We do believe that God made woman and man as a self-expression of divine and undeserved love. God made the universe and everything in it not out of divine need but out of desire for our happiness. We are meant to grow and develop and have our being in God's creation. To safeguard against us feeling like pawns, God gave us the gifts of consciousness and free will to make choices —opening up even the possibility of our choosing against God.

It is no accident that the name of Truman's escape boat is the Santa Maria—the ship Columbus captained in 1492. Columbus took the risk of falling off the edge of the world. We believe God's greatest enjoyment is to be our companion as we explore the many horizons of our world, becoming the men and women God created us to be.

Questions

- What are the trends you see in TV and movies today? What influence can the average viewer have on what is shown?

- What light does the Christian understanding of the relationship between the Creator and creation shed on that of Christof and Truman?

- What is the reality that "reality shows" depict?

The Insider

Starring Al Pacino, Russell Crowe, and Christopher Plummer. Directed by Michael Mann. Rated R. 157 minutes. 1999.

Teachable moments: truth, greed, courage.

Dr. Jeffrey Wigand is a research scientist at tobacco giant Brown & Williamson. Tobacco companies have lied for decades about the addictive nature of their products. Wigand knows this because his job is to manipulate the content of cigarettes so that they function as "a delivery device for nicotine." What makes this story doubly compelling is that it is based on actual events from 1994.

Brown & Williamson become aware that they have lost Wigand's affections and they let him go. But first they tie him to a confidentiality agreement linked to his family's medical coverage. For a father with an asthmatic son, this matters. When the tobacco company starts to worry that Wigand might still go public, they threaten his safety.

At the edge of his nerves, Wigand secretly approaches the producer of *60 Minutes*, Lowell Bergman, and tells what he knows "off the record." Unhappily, Wigand's name leaks out, and his whole family is endangered. His marriage falls apart. With little left to lose, Wigand risks contempt of court and agrees to go on the record. *60 Minutes* bags one of the biggest stories of the decade. But before it airs, CBS's parent company, Westinghouse, objects to the segment, and it is withdrawn. With Wigand betrayed, Bergman sets out to shame CBS into broadcasting the truth.

A good film gives the viewer something important to consider in the opening sequences: background information about the characters, or an image helpful for interpreting the story. *The Insider* opens in Beirut, where Bergman is producing a segment about militant extremists who take Western hostages for ransom. Bergman and host Mike Wallace risk their lives to bring this story out. On one level these scenes portray brave journalists doing an outstanding job in the name of truth. They also set up the narrative: truth has been taken hostage, and one needs the courage of the martyrs to seek it out and speak it.

Christians believe that, in some circumstances, the truth is absolute and not up for grabs. St. Thomas Aquinas, thirteenth-century Dominican theologian, wrote in his poem "Adoro Te," "What God's Son has told me, take for truth I do; / Truth Himself speaks truly or there's nothing true." Democracies debate what the public has a right to know and when, but accountability and transparency are essential foundations of government "of the people, by the people, for the people."

In *The Insider*, the obstacle to the truth is greed. In the Christian tradition, greed is one of the seven deadly sins. Greed deadens us to the call of the truth. It distorts what we hear and have the courage to say. We can be bullied into silence with rewards for colluding with a lie or frightened by the consequences of the truth. The tobacco companies deny the truth because profits will fall. CBS doesn't want the truth to come out because Big Tobacco might withdraw their advertising. Mike Wallace hesitates because he might lose his job.

But some willingly accept the consequences of truth telling because living with its compromise would be far worse. In the Old Testament, such people were called prophets. In the Christian tradition they are martyrs. Wigand does not show perfect resolve, but sometimes imperfect will do: "There are times when I wish I hadn't done it. There are times when I feel compelled to do it. If you asked me, would I do it again, do I think it's worth it? Yeah, I think it's worth it."

Questions

• How can greed deafen us to the call of truth?

• Why was Jeffrey Wigand so reluctant to speak up?

• Can you identify any issues today that need an "insider" to step up and speak out?

The Exorcist

Starring Linda Blair, Max von Sydow, and Ellen Burstyn. Directed by William Friedkin. Rated R. 122 minutes. 1973.

Teachable moments: nature of evil.

Twelve-year-old Regan MacNeil exhibits behavior that is increasingly bizarre and violent. Convinced her daughter is possessed by the devil, Chris MacNeil seeks an exorcist. This film, recut since its debut, remains a shocking story many find distasteful. *The Exorcist* spawned the devil-possession industry. At last count there were more than 250 films about Satan taking up residence in human beings and their homes, including sequels to *The Exorcist, The Omen* series, *Stigmata,* and *The Amityville Horror.* These films exhibit Rudolph Otto's "*mysterium tremendum et fascinans*"—an overwhelming mysterious presence that both repels and attracts. They appear to depict how evil works in the world. The pity is that they are theological rubbish.

The Exorcist takes the reality of evil seriously. So it should. Evil exists. If I can surrender to goodness because of free will, I can also choose to embrace evil. *The Exorcist*, however, presents an innocent person "taken over" by the devil. The possession genre has traded on this scenario ever since. Let's recap: the devil "enters" Regan when she starts playing with the Ouija board in the basement where the pubescent girl, growing up in a dysfunctional home, meets the devil as a friendly older male, Captain Howdy. So far so stupid, but then the rot sets in.

As a result of these casual encounters, Regan is possessed—in the grossest and most highly sexualized way. When she pleads for release, it only gets worse. This is sensational nonsense. If it were true, Christians should be on their knees every morning praying to God that any flirtations with evil might not turn into full-scale possession by lunchtime.

With respect to my fellow Jesuits who consulted on *The Exorcist*, they were wrong if they advised that a person can be possessed against his or her will. Catholics once believed that; those involved in the 1949 case of possession upon which the film is based certainly did. But belief in random possession is prescientific, blaming the devil for everything not understood, from epilepsy to earthquakes. Recent theology emphasizes the agency of free will. Mainstream Christians today consider possession to be rare indeed, and then only as the culmination of deliberate choices for evil. Evil has a context, pattern, and history. Curiously, though we believe good is more powerful than evil, no one makes films about an evil person waking up one day and, completely against his or her will, being possessed by goodness, light, and love.

If *The Exorcist* is nonsense, what do we believe about evil? All people are created in the image of God. Goodness is therefore our natural disposition. Because of free will and original sin, we can make decisions to give ourselves over to violence and destruction. We don't have to go to the basement to find evil; we can look into our own hearts. Though God permits evil to exist—else we would be God's perfect marionettes—God's assistance to ward off evil and choose good is always and everywhere available to us.

In *The Monstrous-Feminine: Film, Feminism, Psychoanalysis*, Barbara Creed argues that horror films regularly misuse women and their sexuality. The genre presents woman as monstrous because she gives birth. In *The Exorcist*, Regan literally embodies evil: the devil resides in her; she becomes physically and spiritually monstrous; and she gives birth to evil, killing two men and leading another to suicide. *The Exorcist* is a profoundly sexist film. Evil deserves a more serious treatment.

Questions

- Even though evil is sensationally portrayed in *The Exorcist*, anecdotally, it's been said that this film may have caused more people to go back to church than any other movie Hollywood has produced. Why do you think that people would say this?

- Does *The Exorcist* portray real evil as it exists in the world around us or does it portray a kind of Hollywood cartoon evil?

Billy Elliot

Starring Julie Walters, Jamie Bell, and Gary Lewis. Directed by Stephen Daldry. Rated R. 110 minutes. 2000.

Teachable moments: vocation, image of the male, image of God, incarnation.

The Elliots have worked in the mines for generations. Young Billy is an anomaly in this environment—a boy for whom boxing, the other family tradition, is a hopeless proposition. In the hall where he takes boxing lessons, girls study ballet with Mrs. Wilkinson. One day after his lesson, Billy stays behind and joins the ballet class. He has natural poise, energy, and expression. But he feels like a sissy.

When the miners go on strike, tensions rise in the Elliot house. Jackie Elliot discovers his son has taken up ballet, and he forbids Billy to dance. Billy disobeys, and Mrs. Wilkinson garners an audition for Billy at a prestigious ballet school in London.

Jackie must choose whether to support his son's ventures into a foreign world or to hold on to the life he knows and insist Billy do the same.

Father-son relationships assume great importance. An absent father can leave a boy without a role model of masculinity, yet for some, the experience of being fathered is likewise inadequate. *Billy Elliot* puts these issues on the screen. When Billy rejects the straightjacket of masculine stereotypes around him, Jackie defaults to thinking his son is homosexual. In County Durham, that charge is as bad as it gets. By choosing dance, Billy demands that his father let him live his own life. The best sort of parenting is when the "chip off the old block" is allowed to be of a completely different grain.

Awareness of masculine stereotypes alerts us also to the patriarchal nature of traditional religious language. Our experiences of being fathered on earth can provide difficulties in relating to the heavenly Father. Unquestionably, we have overdone the father language in theology and liturgy. As privileged as some metaphors may be, no one name, idea, or image sums up who God is. When we pray to God as father, we intend the perfect father—liberating, empowering, nurturing, and protective. The same holds when we pray to God as mother or Jesus as brother. These images are intended to be correctives to what may have been deficient personal experiences of being fathered, mothered, or brothered. The relationship we most need in our lives is the way in which God is with us.

Billy is contrasted sharply with his father—until they go to London together, and we discover how similar they are. Under pressure at the audition, Billy's first instinct is to take flight. As the situation deteriorates, he resorts to verbal and physical violence. We have seen these traits in Jackie. What wins out in the end is that Jackie is prepared to risk everything so that his son can have the chance to fulfill his potential. At the audition, Billy is asked the pivotal question, "What does it feel like when you dance?" He stammers in reply: "I dunno . . . I, I disappear . . . I feel a whole charge in me body . . . like electricity."

Billy's experience of dance is what we hope for in religious experience. Christianity, rooted in the Incarnation, must be embodied. When we communicate with God, we might hope to feel an incarnate "electricity." In *Letters to a Young Poet*, Rainer Maria Rilke advises, "Ask yourself in the stillest hours of your night: must I write? . . . Then build your life according to this necessity." What Rilke asks of poetry, Billy answers in ballet. We are challenged to ask the same question: must I believe?

Questions

- What issues around the development of one's personal vocation does this movie raise? How are they resolved?

- How does Billy's passionate pursuit of dancing ultimately lead his father to freedom?

- How is Billy's experience of dance similar to a religious experience?

Erin Brockovich

Starring Julia Roberts, Albert Finney, and Aaron Eckhart. Directed by Steven Soderbergh. Rated R. 130 minutes. 2000.

Teachable moments: prophecy, anger, temperance.

Erin is a fighter. She speaks before she thinks and regularly offends people. When Erin loses a lawsuit regarding a car accident, she ends up working for her lawyer, Ed Masry. Predictably, Erin alienates everyone at the firm, until she notices a claim involving the Pacific Gas & Electric (PG&E) Company. Her investigation uncovers a toxic-waste dump around which residents suffer a variety of life-threatening illnesses. Erin convinces Masry to fight one of the largest class-action suits ever brought in the United States. This comes at a high cost: to her family life and to his financial solvency.

Erin Brockovich is a modern prophet in the Old Testament style. We may sanitize the ancient prophets, imagining them with long white beards calling forth fire from the mountaintops. In fact, they were the political activists of their day. Moses confronts Pharaoh and demands freedom for his people. Amos rails against corrupt political and religious leaders. Hosea uses the carrot and the stick to persuade Israel to be faithful. Isaiah demands that his king avoid treaties with foreign powers and trust in the Lord. Jeremiah warns his king that unless he reforms his rule, Jerusalem is jeopardized. Finally, Ezekiel warns that the price of ignoring Jeremiah is that justice will visit—soon, and how. Prophecy is hardly religious fortune-telling. Prophets were engaged with the powers that be and were often despised, rejected, and thought to be insane. Israel regularly "shot the messenger."

What Erin has in common with these prophets is holy anger. When the PG&E lawyers offer a settlement of $20 million, Erin is outraged for her humble clients: "These people don't dream about being rich. They dream about being able to watch their kids swim in a pool without worrying that they'll have to have a hysterectomy at the age of twenty. Like Rosa Diaz, a client of ours. Or have their spine deteriorate, like Stan Blume, another client of ours." She adds, "I want you to think real hard about what your spine is worth, Mr. Walker. Or what you might expect someone to pay you for your uterus, Ms. Sanchez. Then you take out your calculator and you multiply that number by a hundred. Anything less than that is a waste of our time."

Anger is a necessary emotion that tells us something is wrong and gives us energy to do something about it. It can be a passionate life force, which is why great art has been created in response to outrage. When we ignore or repress anger, it does not go away.

It reappears elsewhere, demanding attention and action. But anger has a dark side too. It is one of the seven deadly sins with good cause. People who find no constructive use for their anger are consumed by it.

Like the prophets of old, Erin was angry, but she found a way to use it for the good of others. This redemption of her anger makes it holy anger, an impetus for justice. Erin also learns that to achieve her ends, she has to modify her behavior. This is called temperance, a Christian virtue.

Our problem with anger and prophecy is that they don't come gift wrapped. Truth telling can be raw and ugly, in us or in those who sense injustice. One thing is certain: we must heed the warnings of the prophets in our midst. For God still raises them up—whether we want them or not.

Questions

• Who are the prophets in our midst today?

• What is the relationship between anger and justice?

• What stereotypes of women in the marketplace does Erin Brokovich unmask?

Gladiator

Starring Russell Crowe, Joaquin Phoenix, Oliver Reed, Derek Jacobi, Richard Harris, and Connie Neilsen. Directed by Ridley Scott. Rated R. 155 minutes. 2000.

Teachable moments: honor, virtue, faith, afterlife.

The mainstays of the 1950s to mid-1960s cinematic golden age were the epics: *Spartacus, Pompeii, Barabbas, Ben Hur,* and *The Robe.* Such films kept a generation enthralled and pretended to re-create ancient Rome. We believed them. *Gladiator* strives to be a successor to this tradition, particularly in not letting the truth stand in the way of a good story.

Gladiator recounts that in AD 180, while waging a bloody campaign in Germania, Emperor Marcus Aurelius is so pleased with his general Maximus that he wants to bypass his son Commodus's accession and anoint Maximus as emperor. Commodus, enraged, kills his father, Maximus's wife and son, and arranges for the general's death as well. Maximus escapes the assassins but ends up enslaved and purchased for a troupe of gladiators at the Roman Colosseum. Eventually, Commodus is challenged to duel with Maximus.

This story is not true, not even vaguely so. No Roman General Maximus ended up a gladiator. Marcus Aurelius never saw the Germanian front, and the Romans won few battles there until the third century. Commodus was born "to the purple" of a reigning emperor, and was the only son to survive childhood, but he did not murder his father. Marcus died of the plague, but he did live to see Commodus's accession to the throne. Commodus was not a popular emperor, and he did arrange for months of gladiatorial games at the Colosseum to distract the public from his maladministration. He did not, however, enter the arena. He was murdered in bed in a political coup. So let's agree that *Gladiator* is a complete fiction dressed up to look like history.

Two themes make *Gladiator* stand out from its predecessors. The first is the explicit theological thread running throughout the story. While not a Christian, Maximus is a deeply religious man. He seeks to live a life pleasing to the gods. He regularly prays, thanking his ancestor gods for his safety and victory in battle. This firm belief in the gods is amplified by Maximus's belief in the afterlife. Indeed, the tagline of this film is, "What we do in life echoes in eternity." Despite the crimes committed against Maximus, this honorable man has an unfailing belief in the goodness of the gods. Christians can readily identify with his steadfastness.

The second theme, life as journey, dominates the story. References to the journey homeward are everywhere. In the first instance, going home is given as an incentive for battle. Later, the old emperor asks Maximus, "When was the last time you were home?" Maximus reports meaningfully, "Two years, two hundred and sixty-four days, and this morning."

When Maximus's earthly home and family are destroyed, he sets his sights on the final journey home. As he lies dying on the floor of the Colosseum, Lucilla bids him, "Go to them." The gladiator finds his wife and son watching on the road for his return. The film ends with the view tilted up toward the sky.

The path of retribution that marks the last stages of Maximus's earthly journey can hardly be reclaimed by Christian ethics, but many of his values find an easy echo in the cardinal virtues of the Christian tradition recorded in the eighth chapter of the Book of Wisdom: "wisdom, justice, fortitude, and temperance." May our journeys be marked by such virtues, and in place of retribution, may we be forgiving. Then will we be welcomed home by Christ among our honorable ancestors.

Questions

• What strengthens you to live a life of virtue and honor as Maximus did?

• How does our Christian belief in life after death influence how we live our daily lives?

• How does the theme of "life as journey" find an echo in your own experience?

Chocolat

Starring Juliette Binoche, Johnny Depp, Alfred Molina, and Judi Dench.
Directed by Lasse Hallström. Rated PG-13. 121 minutes. 2000.

Teachable moments: Lent, law, change, constancy.

The mayor of a small French town strictly controls his munici-pality. Everyone is expected to attend church, observe the rules, and account for themselves. Dissenters are excommunicated from the church and banished to the fringe of society. During Lent, Vianne and her daughter arrive in town. Vianne opens a chocolate shop, dispensing sweets and wisdom, and providing a listening ear. The comte, or mayor, resents the interloper, who does not go to Mass, but does not consider her and her truffles much of a challenge.

Outcasts are attracted to the shop as a refuge. Josephine is a victim of domestic violence. Armande is an eccentric whose daughter, Caroline, will not let her son Luc have anything to do with his grandmother. The chocolate shop brings grandmother and grandson together. When a traveling band arrives by riverboat, the charismatic Vianne meets her match in Roux, their leader. Roux ignites within Vianne feelings she has long suppressed. Her instinct is to flee, but her time in the village has changed her. She discovers the courage to stay put and build a life.

French films have long employed a form of magical realism called the *cinéma fantastique*, of which *Chocolat* is an example. Fantasy aside, this film says much about issues in the real world. It is a strong criticism of how God may be hijacked to support social repression. The comte's theocracy enforces public propriety. The church serves only to justify the righteous. Despite the efforts of the young priest, this leadership sucks the life out of the community. Père Henri voices his objection: "I think we can't go around measuring our goodness by what we don't do— by what we deny ourselves, what we resist, and who we exclude. I think we've got to measure goodness by what we embrace, what we create, and who we include."

Vianne enters this straightlaced society like a shaman. Shamans are charismatic figures believed to have special insights and healing powers. Against the stifling puritanism of the comte, she sets people free by helping them face their lives, thus facilitating healing. Shamanic religion celebrates freedom from form and structure. *Chocolat* provides not just one but two shamans. For just as Vianne comes to the village on the wind, Roux comes in via another element—water. He offers Vianne what she gives to others. Through Roux, Vianne realizes that there is a better way to overcome her grief than the geographical cure offered by her restless wanderings.

Though critical of organized religion, *Chocolat* is a sacramental film. Sacraments ritualize moments of change. Water, bread, wine, oil, light, rings, gestures, words, and dress symbolize the changes they signify. This film uses chocolate in a similar way, its properties cloaked in mystery. But for those who come to share in the sweet meal at Vianne's table, memories are evoked, stories are told, and community is created.

The allegory with the Eucharist is fairly clear, especially as it becomes evident that Vianne, who presides over the shop, is herself a wounded healer. She often romantically describes the north wind blowing, but we come to see that the wind, related to the Spirit's action in Scripture, has been driving her rather than drawing her. It takes another celebrant of life to help Vianne resist the winds of change and seek a home at last. The Spirit comes to "comfort the afflicted and afflict the comfortable." The veneer of tranquility cannot replace the real thing. Stability and constancy are often the sweetest signs of the Spirit's movement.

Questions

• What issues does this film raise about hypocrisy in religion?

• How does Lent become a season for growth and conversion for the townspeople of Lansquenet?

• What are the challenges to internalizing the spirit of religious practices?

The Lord of the Rings Trilogy

The Fellowship of the Ring
Rated PG-13. 178 minutes. 2001.

The Two Towers
Rated PG-13. 179 minutes. 2002.

The Return of the King
Rated PG-13. 201 minutes. 2003.

Starring Elijah Wood, Ian McKellan, Viggo Mortensen, Sean Astin, Liv Tyler, and Christopher Lee. Screenplay written, produced, and directed by Peter Jackson.

Teachable moments: good and evil, discernment.

Some Christians object to stories about wizards, elves, and dwarfs. For those who take evil seriously, such objections are nonsensical. I only hope those who get into a lather over the evil of fictitious creatures are equally committed to the anything-but-fictional fight against starvation and the unjust distribution of wealth. J. R. R. Tolkien wrote his famous trilogy as a statement of Christian faith in response to the horror of the First World War. A philologist and medieval scholar at Oxford, Tolkien considered his work a parable about the forces of light and darkness.

The plot centers on the One Ring of Power, thought to be lost for many years. It was made by the Dark Lord Sauron, who intends to dominate Middle Earth with it. When a hobbit, Frodo, inherits the ring, the wizard Gandalf instructs him that the ring must be destroyed at Mount Doom. In this quest they are joined by three hobbits, an elf, a dwarf, and two men. This group comprises the unlikely Fellowship.

In *The Two Towers*, the Fellowship protecting Frodo is shattered. Gandalf is believed dead. The two hobbits Frodo and Samwise go on alone to destroy the ring. An earlier ring bearer named Gollum follows the hobbits to recapture his "precious" ring. The hobbits compel Gollum to guide them to Mount Doom. In *Return of the King*, Gollum gains Frodo's trust. Samwise is harder to persuade. Sam's suspicions tear the two friends apart. Meanwhile a restored Gandalf convinces the leader of Middle Earth that the hour for battle has arrived. The renewed Fellowship confronts the encroaching dark forces. Hopelessly outnumbered, they gain the advantage when Frodo achieves his destiny and destroys the ring. Gandalf crowns Aragorn, protector of the Fellowship, the new king.

The Lord of the Rings may be an allegory on the reign of Christ the King. Tolkien, a veteran of war, believed that some battles are necessary to defeat evil. Another approach to these films is through the Christ figures. There are at least three: Gandalf, who dies and rises; Frodo, who travels the Via Dolorosa with the ring; and Aragorn, the hidden king finally revealed in triumph. Galadriel may be seen as the mother of God, reflecting Tolkien's deep Marian devotion. Alternatively, we have a reimaging of the Trinity: Gandalf, the father who creates and calls; Frodo, the son who bears the form of the least but whose destiny is to save; and Galadriel, the spirit who inspires, enlightens, and comforts.

This story is also a study in discernment. Consider the climb to Mount Doom. Frodo must learn whether to listen to Samwise or Gollum as Gollum tempts Frodo to pride, power, and greed. Gollum, who was once the hobbit Smeagol, is already a victim to the very temptations he offers to Frodo. Blinded by fatigue and desire, Frodo has to march on not knowing which voice to follow.

Meanwhile, Aragorn and Gandalf must discern whether Frodo is still alive before mounting an attack on Mordor. "What does your heart tell you?" Aragorn asks. Taking stock of their hearts, they enter into the final battle. Heart, mind, and body are all part of their discernment. These, as the mystical tradition of the church attests, are the fundamental things upon which Christian discernment is built.

Questions

• Why did Tolkien choose Frodo as the hero of his epic fantasy story?

• In a society based on science and technology, what value is placed on knowing one's heart?

• How is the Christian practice of discernment inclusive of the whole person (body, mind, and spirit)?

Glory

Starring Matthew Broderick, Denzel Washington, and Morgan Freeman.
Directed by Edward Zwick. Rated R. 122 minutes. 1989.

Teachable moments: war, trust, glory.

During the Civil War, young Bostonian Robert Shaw volunteered to lead the first regiment of African American troops in the Union's history. His battalion was composed of volunteers who wanted to fight for the Union and for emancipation. During their preparation, Shaw wrote letters to his mother that now provide a poignant window on history.

Thomas Searles, a free man of color and Shaw's friend, is the first volunteer. Being Shaw's subordinate is challenging. The educated Searles must adjust not only to army discipline, but also to racism from fellow infantrymen, who label him "Snowflake." Other Union soldiers do not take the troop seriously as a fighting force, and the new soldiers are not adequately paid or provided for. The

Southern army resolves to kill the regiment and its leaders without provocation. To gain respect, Shaw volunteers to lead his men in the assault on Fort Wagner. The 54th Regiment faces certain death.

Glory is an intelligent film that does not hide from the ambiguities involved in the creation of heroes. From an outsider's perspective, army discipline can appear aimed more at the disintegration of personalities than at saving lives. In *Glory* we see how it also instills confidence, forms the group's identity, and establishes routines that protect the soldiers. At its best, discipline is tough love. *Glory* explores the many faces of racism and how all those infected with its virus become victims. The most challenging and racist dialogue in the film is spoken not by white soldiers to black, but between African American soldiers. *Glory* walks the wartime tightrope of whether troops are brave or stupid to march into insurmountable odds. Are the 54th Regiment civil saints because they were the first black company or because they were used as cannon fodder? There is something sacred about the trust between a soldier and his or her commanding officer. The responsibility of leading troops is a grave one as well.

Christianity has a special reverence for glory. We believe the glory of God is manifest in the Word made flesh. Jesus glorified our humanity by the way he lived and died as one of us. He was raised up to live in glory, and in the power of the Holy Spirit we glimpse the glory to which we are destined. Glory is revealed in the outpouring of God's life to us in Christ, from Christ to us in the Spirit, from us to one another in God. Glory enables us to offer everything we have in establishing the kingdom of heaven. That's why the 54th and the one hundred eighty thousand African American troops who turned the tide of the Civil War are glorious men. They held nothing back to fight the tyranny of repression. Nor should we.

On the eve of the assault, the spiritual leader of the regiment, Jupiter, helps the soldiers tell their stories. As in our Liturgy of the Word, we hear of the deeds of men, of their struggles and anxieties, as they participate in creating a better world. Trip sums up the hour: "Yall's the onliest family I got. I love the 54th. Ain't even much a matter what happens tomorrow, 'cause we men, ain't we?" Human dignity is not focused on death, but on life. It reminds me of what another saint said in the second century. This one is canonized, St. Irenaeus: "The glory of God is humanity fully alive." In the battle of life as elsewhere, no guts, no glory.

Questions

• What is the "price" of glory for the soldiers in this movie?

• How does the sharing of personal stories mold individuals into a community?

• How does racism continue to be an issue in our country, church, and neighborhoods today?

Bowling for Columbine

Documentary film narrated by Michael Moore. Directed by Michael Moore. Rated R. 120 minutes. 2002.

Teachable moments: violence, fear, responsibility.

This controversial film asks an important question: why does the United States have the greatest number of gun-related deaths in the world? Moore focuses on the day when two American teenagers walked into Columbine High School and gunned down fellow students and teachers. Moore wonders why the U.S. was the only industrialized country in the world to have anywhere near 11,127 gun-related deaths in 2001. The next highest total is 381 in Germany. It is a staggering difference.

Moore unpacks the usual arguments, such as the ease of gun access in the U.S. Canada, however, has more guns per capita than the U.S., seven million guns for ten million people, but had only 165 gun-related deaths in 2001. Other arguments are advanced: American history, engagement in wars around the world, media influence. Yet comparable countries have worse histories, engagements, and similar exposure to media, without the appalling statistics.

Moore posits that combined with these factors is fear, the driving force in American society. Citizens are told early and often that they should be frightened, that their lives, liberty, and possessions are in danger from local criminals (defined by racial profiling) as well as international terrorists. Such a climate breeds a "shoot first, ask questions later" mentality, hiding behind a faulty interpretation of the constitutional right to bear arms.

With *Bowling for Columbine, Sicko, Fahrenheit 9/11, Pets or Meat: The Return to Flint,* and *Roger and Me,* Moore put the documentary back on the big screen, proving they can make money—and stir up controversy. We already know when we go to his films what we will get: a merciless attack on an issue in the public domain. Moore believes one side of the debate has been already well aired and that it is time to gather forces for the opposite position. The best documentary films are subjective, intending to persuade the viewer of their perspectives. Everyone pushes a barrow, even if they pretend otherwise. Rather than be resentful of Moore and his colleagues, his critics should be grateful for the freedom of speech they exercise and mount an engaging counterattack.

The thesis in *Bowling for Columbine* has deep resonances in the biblical tradition. Throughout the Bible we are told to be fearful of the Lord. In a few places this means that we should be apprehensive in regard to God's judgment. God takes seriously what we do to each other, and this life has a critical bearing on eternal life as well. Fear of the Lord is also used in the sense of being filled with wonder and awe at the greatness of God. In the New Testament, however, Jesus regularly counsels disciples not to be afraid of him, or others, or the world. "Perfect love casts out fear," St. Paul tells us (1 John 4:18). While we respect God and others, fearlessness is one mark of a Christian.

Fearlessness, however, is different than stupidity. The virtue of courage includes assessing the danger, being prepared, and not taking unnecessary risks. Moore claims we are being conditioned to be afraid. The best Christian response to the scapegoating and racist profiling that accompanies these bleak social assessments is to educate ourselves as fully as possible. It is possible to resolve conflicts peacefully. At the same time, we will be asked to account for what we did and what we failed to do about the culture of death in our society.

Questions

- How has fear become a driving force in American culture?

- How do our Christian lives call us to live without fear? What does that look like?

- How does our fascination with guns and violence contribute to the culture of death in our society?

In America

Starring Paddy Considine, Samantha Morton, Djimon Hounsou, Sarah Bolger, and Emma Bolger. Directed by Jim Sheridan. Rated PG-13. 105 minutes. 2002.

Teachable moments: love, acceptance, resurrection.

Johnny and Sarah pack up their daughters, Christy and Ariel and leave the Emerald Isle for the United States, settling in Manhattan. The family carries more baggage than most. Johnny and Sarah lost their son, Frankie, a year earlier. When an immigration officer asks how many children they have, Johnny answers three, Sarah two. Pained, Johnny laments, "We lost one."

The move is a painful flight from grief. But life in the Big Apple is not easy. A tenement in the dodgy end of town is all that an out-of-work actor like Johnny Sheridan can afford. The neighbors seem mad, bad, or ill. Sarah is told her pregnancy is potentially life threatening. Meanwhile Ariel and Christy go trick-or-treating in the building on Halloween. They meet Mateo, an African immigrant dying of AIDS. Although he appears terrifying at first, Mateo cries when the children speak of their dead brother. The girls decide to trust him.

Mateo is a reclusive artist, yet Sarah and the girls become his friends. Johnny, now forced to drive a cab—between auditions—to support his family, resents their closeness. Fearful of losing his family, Johnny asks, "Are you in love with her?" Mateo explodes with passion: "No . . . I'm in love with you. And I'm in love with your beautiful woman. And I'm in love with your kids. And I'm even in love with your unborn child. I'm even in love with your anger! I'm in love with anything that lives!"

In America is an autobiographical work from director Jim Sheridan. But it is also an allegory on the raising of Lazarus in John chapter 11. In the Gospel, Jesus waits before heading to Bethany, where his friend Lazarus has been ill. On arrival Jesus faces Mary and Martha, Lazarus's sisters, who want to know where Jesus was when they needed him most. At the tomb Jesus weeps, prays, and raises Lazarus from the dead. He orders him unbound so he can be united with his family. We soon learn the cost of this episode. As a result of raising Lazarus, Jesus' own life comes under a death sentence.

As in the story of Lazarus, movement is central to this film. The Sheridans travel to New York City to ease the pain, yet each member of the family has to journey farther to heal the past and face the future. When Johnny asks his daughter, "Are you okay little girl?" Christy angrily replies, "Don't 'little girl' me.

I've been carrying this family on my back for over a year, ever since Frankie died. He was my brother too." Even Mateo, who has come from Africa, must journey up the stairs to find new life. In death he finds another stairway to ascend to do more for his newfound friends.

Just as Mary remonstrates with Jesus about his absence from Bethany, the absence of God in this film is palpable too. Because of Frankie's death, Johnny lost his faith in God. Mateo helps Johnny find faith again—in himself, in love, and in God, or at least in miracles. As Sarah's baby fights for life, Mateo goes to his death. He lays down his life, and in doing so "breathes" on the baby. The little boy takes up his life. The family's raw and unresolved grief is finally released. Johnny can finally let Frankie go. As he does, his family welcomes him back from the dead. The journey is over.

Questions

- How does Mateo's death affect Johnny?

- How does the power of love transform the effects of grief and pain on each of the characters in this movie?

- How do children, like Christy, reveal what is often hidden from adults?

Vera Drake

Starring Imelda Staunton, Richard Graham, Eddie Marsan, and Anna Keaveney. Written and directed by Mike Leigh. Rated R. 125 minutes. 2004.

Teachable moments: conscience, sanctity of life.

Vera Drake is a motherly, reassuring presence in a 1950s London housing project. Vera shares what she has with a demanding mother, sick neighbor, and anyone else in need. Vera supplements her husband's wages by cleaning the homes of the wealthy. Vera also "helps young girls out." This is code for performing syringe-flush abortions. The sinister Lily recruits Vera for each task over tea, supplying a name, address, and time. Stealthily, Lily also pockets an abortion fee. In precontraceptive England, Vera breaks the law to "set things right" for girls in "trouble." By contrast, one of Vera's upper-class ladies easily procures an abortion at an exclusive hospital as a "medical emergency."

Not all of Vera's services have the desired outcome. When one abortion goes horribly wrong, the woman almost dies. As a result, Vera is arrested at home. Her family, ignorant of Vera's activities, is stunned by the revelation. Vera goes to trial and is convicted.

Vera Drake is a harrowing example of following an erroneous conscience. Conscience is the forum where we seek truth, deliberate its application, and determine the morality of our actions. John Henry Newman went so far as to say, "I have a conscience, therefore I am a human being," defining conscience as "the aboriginal [or first] vicar of Christ." A Christian conscience is informed by Scripture and church teaching. It also considers civil laws, authorities, and scholars. Our personal gifts, abilities, and life experiences play a pivotal role in the formation of conscience. When we find ourselves in contradiction with church teaching, it may be a result of who we are as much as of our grasp of the teaching. Because of an inability to learn, inexperience, spiritual or emotional immaturity, pride, or stubbornness, we may presume we have fulfilled the obligation to inform our consciences. A limited search for truth may simply reinforce what we wanted to think and do in the first instance.

From the Christian perspective, as well-intentioned as she is, Vera has an objectively erroneous conscience in regard to abortion. In making a judgment about the error in her conscience and the terrible consequences that follow from it, we are in no position to condemn Vera, as Sid initially does. Only God knows her soul and can pass judgment. We see that Vera, limited in formal learning and with an acute ignorance of the results of her actions, does follow her conscience. She helps girls with their "problems."

Most Christians believe that while a mother should receive every support with her pregnancy, the baby is not a "problem" and abortion not an answer.

Vera deals with abortion by inventing another language for it that never names the termination, deals with the fetus tangibly, or follows up with the mother after the abortion. Vera arrives to "set things right," resulting in "it" coming away. Her job done, several times Vera walks away from a frightened woman lying on a bed in tears, in distress—a chronicle of her denial.

Vera leads a double life, one of charity conducted in the light, and another concealed in the dark. As abortion on demand was not legal in the United Kingdom until 1967, Vera's secrecy might be understandable. But there is something compartmentalized about Vera going about her daily rounds, locking and unlocking doors. Right conscience is marked by its transparency to the world and the courage to live with the consequences we create for ourselves and others.

Questions

- How does Vera live a double life?

- Vera twists language to avoid the truth. How does that happen in the media, and in political, religious, and social institutions?

- How is the Christian belief in the sanctity of life reflected in our society today?

The Third Miracle

Starring Ed Harris and Anne Heche. Directed by Agnieszka Holland.
Rated R. 119 minutes. 1999.

Teachable moments: saints, faith.

Fr. Frank Shore is asked to investigate the claim that a recently
deceased woman is a saint. On the anniversary of her death a
statue weeps blood over a young girl, who is then found to be
cured of lupus. Frank is known for exposing fraudulent candi-
dates for sainthood. The problem is, Frank's vocation has been
in crisis ever since the last investigation, as he reminds the
bishop: "I destroyed an entire community's faith." In examin-
ing Helen's case, Frank meets her daughter, Roxane, who rejects
any saintliness in her mother. Roxane claims to have suffered
neglect and abuse. Some martyrs are created when they have to
live with saints. As the investigation ensues, Frank and Roxane
fall in love.

A Vatican delegation arrives, among them a German arch-bishop serving as devil's advocate to debunk Helen's cause. Frank defends it, but faces an insurmountable problem: Helen's cause has produced only two miracles. Will there be a third?

The filmmaker did her homework. The definition of a saint, the need for a local cult, and the reason for miracles are intelli-gently demonstrated. The church does take mysticism seriously but not uncritically. Qualifying for canonization as a mystic is difficult: heroic virtue and martyrdom fare better. In 1979, the setting of the film, Rome required three miracles for a person to be beatified, declared blessed—the step before canonization, when one is declared a saint of the church. In 1979 there was an office of devil's advocate, charged with the argument against the candidate's cause. The need for three miracles and the devil's advocate were abolished in the revised process of 1982. Now, beatification requires one miracle and canonization a further one. No one is invested with discrediting the case.

The film contains some errors. The Vatican does not get directly involved in the cause of a saint at its earliest stages, as Helen's was. It certainly does not send colleges of bishops to sort things out. The occasion is simply provided to present offi-cious bishops strutting their stuff. And when will Hollywood get over its grief that most religious women in the Western world no longer wear veils and wimples?

Saints matter, but not because they do tricks for us. Saints do not perform miracles under their own power. All miracles come from God. Saints demonstrate how human beings can live lives of heroic sacrifice, exceptional goodness, and great holiness. They assure us that amazing grace is active, inspiring us to live ordinary lives extraordinarily well. Miracles are signs that a person enjoys eternal life with God and give us confidence that they remain present to us as friends and companions.

Two public miracles are established for Helen's cause. A third and fourth miracle are evident but not public. The archbishop remembers how, during the war, a young woman prayed for the bombs to stop falling on their town. The girl was Helen, but the archbishop cannot prove the miracle. It is a private revelation for the man fighting her cause. The final miracle occurs when Fr. Frank resumes his ministry with purpose and peace. He meets Roxane, now married and with a child. They seem to testify that finding our purpose and being faithful to it is a daily miracle. Helen's cause for sainthood is abandoned. She may not have been a mystic after all. But when we look for proof of goodness, we may find it—in our lives. All we need are eyes to see it.

Questions

• What is Fr. Frank's miracle in this movie?

• How does the church determine sainthood today?

• What are the gifts that saints offer to us in living our daily lives?

Italian for Beginners

Starring Anders Berthelsen and Peter Gantzler. Directed by Lone Scherfig.
Rated R. 118 minutes. 2000. Danish with English subtitles.

Teachable moments: ministry, church, healing.

Italian for Beginners is a romantic comedy about the lovelorn living in Copenhagen who join an Italian-language class. It begins
with the arrival of Andreas, the acting Lutheran pastor. The previous pastor was sacked after beating up the organist in a dispute
about the speed of the hymns. The new pastor takes up residence
in a hotel because his predecessor refuses to leave the presbytery.
Andreas is befriended by the hotel manager, Jørgen, who is
besotted with Giulia, a barmaid in a nearby restaurant. Hal-finn,
the restaurant manager, blows up at customers who ask for anything that isn't on the menu. Threatened with dismissal for his

attitude and appearance, Hal-finn goes for a haircut from Karen, whose demanding mother dominates her life, and Hal-finn is smitten. Meanwhile, Andreas meets Olympia, whose chronic clumsiness has propelled her through thirty-two jobs. She works in a pastry shop, where the products are unbreakable. Andreas, recovering from the death of his wife, falls for Olympia.

They all end up in Italian class. Hal-finn becomes the teacher. The class decides to practice its newfound language skills with a trip to Venice, and love blossoms in a variety of ways

With humor, this film examines the pain of oppressive parents, poor self-esteem, forgiveness, reconciliation, living with mental illness, failed romances, and whether "mercy killing" is merciful at all. We follow these characters in their searches for love. Hal-finn uses power to get sex, which he mistakes for love, until he actually falls in love. Jørgen thinks he is unlovable, until he discovers Giulia's attraction for him. Andreas doubts if he can love again. And Olympia and Karen battle years of deprivation to realize their self-worth.

Two strong Christian themes arise in this film. The first is how wounded healers minister to each other. In contemporary cinema it is rare to find sympathetic presentations of ministry. Yet the hard old pastor is clearly mentally ill, and his illness has driven his congregation away. Andreas represents the new breed: intelligent, gentle, caring, and needy. He is a minister situated firmly in his community, sharing their joys and hopes, griefs and anxieties. In this context, ministry is mutually empowering. The film is also instructive about how churches must go out to the highways and byways to meet people where they are, as they are.

Andreas inherits a congregation of three. By the end of the film the church is nearly full. His humanity has made room for others where once there had been no room.

Italian for Beginners raises issues about the nature of God. The old pastor's decline and loss of faith began when he lost his wife. Andreas, on the other hand, found his faith a great consolation when his wife died.

The Scriptures emphasize how God regularly arrives in unusual ways, at unlikely times, and through unexpected people. While we look for God in the spectacular, God comes poor, naked, sick, in prison, and hungry. In this film, to find solace these broken people need to learn to love again. It may be a foreign tongue, but everyone can master the language of love.

Love in all its forms—familial, romantic, shared between friends, and spiritual—is a gift from God to form us into being better human beings. Jesuit Fr. Pedro Arrupe summed it up well when he said, "Nothing is more practical than finding God, that is, than falling in love in a quite absolute, final way. . . . Fall in love, stay in love, and it will decide everything."

Questions

- How does the church today reach out to people where they are, as they are?

- Where are some unexpected places in which Christ chooses to reveal himself?

- How does love become the thread that brings healing to the individuals in the film?

Whale Rider

Starring Keisha Castle-Hughes, Rawiri Paratene, and Vicky Haughton.
Directed by Niki Caro. Rated PG-13. 101 minutes. 2002.

Teachable moments: courage, leadership, gender stereotypes.

The Whangara people in New Zealand maintain that their leader Paikea came from Hawaii riding on the back of a whale. Firstborn males of the Paikea clan have led the tribe ever since. Present chief Koro has a son, Porourangi, who rejected tribal life and lives in Germany. As a younger man, Porourangi fathered twins. His wife and baby boy died after childbirth. A girl, Pai, is the only direct descendant.

Pai's grandparents raise her on tribal lands. Koro loves his granddaughter, and she excels in learning tribal traditions, yet he cannot break patriarchal tradition and anoint Pai as chief. Koro seeks a boy worthy of the role. Pai intuits that she is called to lead, and so, with help from her grandmother and some whales, she sets out to prove it.

Some films elicit from viewers a mystical gaze. When people come to the cinema primed for an encounter with otherness—and some directors know how to exploit this predisposition—such viewers report an encounter similar to a mystical experience. For a film to be mystical it requires four elements: the story connects with other spiritual texts explored through the explicit use of symbols; the hero's quest is primarily a spiritual one with which the viewer empathizes; at a critical moment, the viewer is placed in an omnipotent position to preside over the hero's journey; in its artistic use of media and focus on the themes of sexuality, death, and intimacy, the viewer accepts the fluid boundaries between seen and unseen worlds, raising questions about the viewer's own meaning and purpose.

Whale Rider is such a mystical film, containing allegories to the Christian story. The Paikea clan wait for the arrival of a chief who will lead them out of darkness. When the leader comes, she is in an unexpected form. She is therefore rejected by the religious authority of the clan. Pai's ability to commune with the ancestors and her knowledge of tribal ways elevates her above all other claimants to the title. Her identity is revealed in the fearless way she faces death. She is prepared to lay down her life for her people. She gives hope back to them and reconciles ancient beliefs with new possibilities.

For some Christians, women in leadership roles is a vexed issue. Because of the way tradition has been appropriated, women have been excluded from ordination or ministerial commissioning.

This is the bind Koro faces: can the patrilineal line be broken without negative consequences? *Whale Rider* argues that it can.

Leadership is not only defined by official appointment. Women lead at all levels of Christian education, welfare, and health care. Trouble strikes when we think of tradition as static. Adaptations have added to the richness of local cultures, have corrected destructive elements within them, and have enabled both sides to learn from the process. Christian inculturation accepts that Christ is already present in the best of any human community. Tradition is necessarily dynamic and has always been so.

Whale Rider highlights the pain of transition. During the film shoot, many Maori cast and crew members offered up chants to the ancestors for protection because Keisha Castle-Hughes, who played Pai, was performing traditional rituals never undertaken by a woman before. Art imitates life.

Questions

- How does this film highlight the dynamic nature of tradition?

- How does authentic leadership transcend gender?

- How might the story of Pai and her clan be an allegory of the Christian story?

The Hurricane

Starring Denzel Washington, Vicellous Reon Shannon, Deborah Kara Unger,
Liev Schreiber, and John Hannah. Directed by Norman Jewison.
Rated R. 145 minutes. 1999.

Teachable moments: racism, resurrection, desire.

The Hurricane is a masterful study of racism and those who
are entrapped by it. It also explores what constitutes freedom,
the cost of following one's conscience, the cause for justice, the
importance of friendship, and the power of words—written,
read, and spoken. This film purports to tell the story of a man
who could have "been one of the greatest fighters of all time" if
not falsely convicted of murder. We know from later jury inter-
views that Rubin Carter was only spared capital punishment
in 1967 because the jury thought his death might provoke race
riots. Despite the rejections of his appeals, in prison Carter writes
a fateful book putting forward his side of the story. Years after its

publication, Lesra, a struggling young African American, obtains the book. Moved by what he reads, Lesra begins a correspondence with Carter that leads to a fresh campaign for his release.

In cinema studies, much is made of what scholars term "intertextuality"—the process in which a writer makes a point by using an image, name, phrase, speech, or allusion to another text. This other text deepens the meaning of the context in which it is now applied. A significant intertextual motif comes free of charge in the names of the two leading characters. In the Book of Genesis, Reuben, eldest son of Jacob and Leah, is deprived of his birthright because of his previous crimes. This starts him on a violent future, though he does reject killing his brother Joseph. Reuben is guilty of many things, but murder is not one of them. Reuben recovers from his criminal start to become a patriarch of one of the twelve tribes of Israel.

Lesra is a form of Lazarus, whom, in John chapter 11, Jesus raised from the dead: "Unbind him, and let him go" (11:44). In this film the tables are somewhat turned: Rubin Carter sets the thirst for justice free in his young friend, but it is Lesra's hopefulness and hard work that see Carter emerge from his unjust tomb. Carter tells Lesra, "Hate put me in prison, love is gonna bust me out."

The Hurricane makes us conscious of what a tomb racism is. It is filled with death, because no matter what people do, if they are "judged by the color of their skin [rather than] by the content of their character," they are denied opportunity. They are entombed by the color blindness of prejudice. This film also alerts us to the importance of desire. In the desolate years in prison, Rubin takes control of his life by denying himself every small luxury. As he explains, "My own freedom lay in not wanting or needing anything of which they could deprive me." He even divorces his faithful wife, telling her not to visit him. Control borne of resentment exacts a high toll, until Lesra comes to Ruben's sealed tomb and awakens hope in a man left for dead by the world.

Desires, in themselves, are good and God given. They may need focus and discipline, but our desires make us who we are. *The Hurricane* reminds us that it is God's desire to see justice done on earth as a foretaste of what we will enjoy in heaven. The story of Rubin "Hurricane" Carter reminds us that every so often, against impossible odds and through the goodness of human hearts, the reign of God breaks in upon the world.

Questions

- How does racism entomb not only the victim but the perpetrator?

- How are the lives of Rubin and Lesra transformed by the power of the written word?

- How do our desires shape us into who we are? What control do we have over them?

The Crime of
Father Amaro

Starring Gale García Bernal, Ana Claudia Talancón, and Sancho Gracia.
Directed by Carlos Carrera. Rated R. 118 minutes. 2002. Spanish with
English subtitles.

Teachable moments: sexual abuse, misuse of power.

Newly ordained Fr. Amaro is assigned to a small town in the
Mexican mountains. Talented, handsome, and ambitious, the
young priest has already been singled out for a promising future.
Fr. Amaro finds parish life difficult. The pastor, Fr. Benito, pan-
ders to corrupt landowners for financial support. He is also having
an affair with a parishioner. An assistant, Fr. Natalio, ministers
to poor farmers and is suspected of supporting guerrilla troops.

Initially Fr. Amaro wants to keep his head down. But he soon
comes under the charms of sixteen-year-old Amelia, a beautiful

girl with great devotion. Her mother is Fr. Benito's lover. Amelia is entranced by Fr. Amaro, and they begin an affair. Controversy erupts when Fr. Benito accepts drug money for the health center he is building, and Fr. Natalio is condemned for supporting resistance fighters. When Amelia becomes pregnant, Fr. Amaro finds himself holding three futures in his hands.

For many of us, the church is only one of several institutions that inform our culture. Viewers outside Latin countries may not appreciate the power of the church over the people there. Sometimes the church has been complicit against the interests of its people. Anticlericalism runs deep against the church's abuse of power and hypocrisy. Amelia, preyed upon and destroyed in her innocence, represents that hypocrisy at its most sickening.

Christians in recent years have been rocked by scandals concerning priests, ministers, or pastors. We have heard the shameful stories of sexual abuse, financial impropriety, and cover-ups. In this context, *The Crime of Father Amaro* touches a nerve and tells a story important well beyond Mexican borders. Fr. Amaro uses his power to steal a child's innocence. Of particular abhorrence is how he uses piety to seduce Amelia. He blesses her, dresses her in religious accessories, and quotes the Song of Songs to justify his behavior. Sexual abuse always has a personal and institutional context. It is as much about power as it is about sex. Fr. Amaro is the blue-eyed darling of the diocese, destined to teach others about ethics and morality. Yet the models of priesthood around him are appalling. Fr. Benito is not celibate and courts the cartels. The bishop is arrogant, conceited, and pampered. Fr. Galván is an alcoholic. The noblest priest, Fr. Natalio, is sincerely committed to the poor, but his support of violent retribution cannot be reconciled with the gospel.

Within such a fraudulent culture, Fr. Amaro's deceit flourishes. Celibacy gets the blame for driving good men to do bad things. The fact that the greatest amount of sexual abuse occurs in the family home is not acknowledged. The wider context—a lack of accountability and transparency, an overly sexualized society, spiritual malaise, and the abuse of power—are more serious elements in understanding sexual abuse than are portrayed here.

When Amelia becomes pregnant, Amaro's first instincts are to protect his future. Morally bankrupt, he views Amelia and their child as problems to be dealt with. After an abortion, Amelia hemorrhages to death. Teenage mother and her child are both victims of Amaro's vanity. *The Crime of Father Amaro* painfully demonstrates that the wages of sin is death. May the repentance we see in the young priest at the end of the film be a sign of a broader social and ecclesiastical conversion. The sufferings of victims of abuse, and the many forms of death they have endured, demand nothing less.

Questions

• How does false piety distort authentic religious practice?

• How does this film depict the interrelationship between sex and power?

• What are the deeper issues that the sexual abuse scandal in the church has brought to light?

Finding Nemo

Animation film voiced by Albert Brooks, Ellen DeGeneres, Alexander Gould, Barry Humphries, Willem Dafoe, and Geoffrey Rush. Directed by Andrew Stanton and Lee Unkrich. Rated G. 100 minutes. 2003.

Teachable moments: freedom, responsibility.

When Nemo is just a baby, his clown-fish mother sacrifices her life to save him from the sharks. Racked by guilt and anxiety, Nemo's father, Marlin, becomes overly protective of his son. He vows never to let anything happen to him. A funny thing to promise, as another fish points out.

Eventually, Marlin allows Nemo to go to school. On the first day, Nemo is caught by a scuba diver and sold to a Sydney dentist who collects exotic fish for his office aquarium. Marlin is broken-hearted and sets out to find his son. Early on, Dory, a memory-challenged angelfish, joins him in his search. They venture across the Pacific Ocean to rescue Nemo, who has entered the strange world of the fish tank. Life in the fish tank is defined by the yearning to escape.

In this warm and engaging film, all manner of human behavior is gently held up for exploration, parody, and celebration, even the famous 12-Step programs, which have done so much good for so many. At its heart, *Finding Nemo* is a parable about letting go. Marlin needs to allow his son to venture forth. In turn, Nemo comes to value what he's taken for granted: the security of a loving home. Parents have no greater fear than allowing their children to venture out into the world, especially if they are ill prepared for what they might encounter.

Christianity has had a variable relationship with the world. At times the world has been viewed as a hostile place with temptations and risks to the life of faith. This is the Marlin school of theology—venture out only when necessary, and then do so with extreme vigilance. Like Marlin, Christians who approach society like this usually have a wound behind their bleak assessment of the world. Monasteries were once the refuge for the cautious believer when safety was the name of the faith game.

The Nemo school of theology holds that the world is the gift of God, to be explored, dealt with, delighted in, and within which we learn who we are and who God is in the scheme of things. Both schools of theology live side by side in the church and are often the source of tension.

St. Ignatius of Loyola thought about this tension more than most. In the 1530s, when monastic power was at its height, Ignatius discerned that the church needed to go out and meet the rapidly changing Renaissance world. Since God had created the world and placed us in it with the gift of free will, then with the appropriate safeguards of prayer, learning, leadership, and friends, we might confidently be in the world as well

For Christians, God can be found in everything, except evil. We were not created to be God's marionettes, simply dancing to his tune. Free will is a richer gift than that. Christ sends us out to swim among the sharks with gifts of intelligence, prudence, wisdom, and self-control. And even though God might sometimes despair of the warning signs we often ignore, he also delights when we discover within us his creativity, ingenuity, and passion. And as Marlin and Nemo discover, we are never swimming alone. We have the community of faith to lead us, pray with us, teach us, and be our friends in the Lord. Or as the sharks might say, "We're all mates here."

Questions

• How do Nemo's and Marlin's outlooks on life differ? What is the tension that arises when the two outlooks collide?

• How does Nemo learn that freedom comes with responsibility?

• As disciples sent by Christ into the world, how are we invited to "find God in all things"?

Bruce Almighty

Starring Jim Carrey, Jennifer Aniston, and Morgan Freeman. Directed by Tom Shadyac. Rated PG-13. 101 minutes. 2003.

Teachable moments: nature of God, humility, free will.

Bruce Nolan is a television reporter. He gets the soft news stories at the end of the broadcast. His ambition is to be anchorman. While his girlfriend, Grace, prays that Bruce gets the job, the station appoints his archrival. Bruce explodes on air, loses his job, and blames God. God appears and challenges Bruce to do a better job at presiding over the world. There's a catch: "You have to learn the rules." Bruce discovers that being divine is not as easy as he thought.

Bruce acts out humanity's most ancient desire—to be God. The original sin is not that Adam and Eve ate the fruit of the forbidden tree, but that they desired to gain what the serpent promised: to be like God, "able to know right from wrong." Original sin is this rejection of our creatureliness to compete with our Creator, to be God. The desire to be God encompasses much aberrant behavior. Some people become control freaks, manipulating everything and everyone so that no self-respecting surprise would dare show its dynamic face. Other people worship themselves, their money, beauty, or power. Such narcissism makes God over in our own image and likeness. Bruce discovers that being God is not about absolute power, but about how to control absolute power.

At first Bruce enjoys the gimmicks of being God. He parts the "red sea" of his tomato soup. He gets Grace to marry him and house-trains the dog. He gains respect at work by making his rival look stupid. Bruce carelessly grants all the prayers of the world, even those that rule each other out. Bruce, our self-centered god, is soon presiding over chaos. He did not respect the rules.

Bruce Almighty suggests that God operates on two fundamental principles: "You can't mess with free will," and "You can't do everything." Christian theology teaches that God is omnipotent (all-powerful), omniscient (all-knowing), omnipresent (all-present), and all-loving. *Bruce Almighty* gives this a contemporary spin. Rather than positing a God deficient in power, it suggests God has a self-imposed limit on the exercise of power. A helpful analogy is that of parents and their children. Out of love, some parents want to control their children completely—to know everything, do everything, and be everything for them. Their motivation may be benign but this behavior can result in disaster for the child. Children controlled like this do not mature, learn their limits, realize their potential, or develop their gifts. The all-powerful parent is not nurturing, but smothering. God nurtures us rather than smothers us.

The film raises interesting issues and images. The first concerns prayer: do our prayers change God or us? This film demonstrates the first approach to prayer and ends up endorsing the latter. Not for nothing is Bruce's girlfriend named *Grace*, that ancient word for the undeserved movement of God's love. Finally, truth tellers in this film are invariably the poor. To experience the abundant life of grace we need to stay close to the poor.

This romantic comedy does not have the nuance many will want in public theological debate. But it gets points for trying. It attempts to ask the most basic religious questions in a modern context and with humor. *Bruce Almighty* helps us reclaim laughter as an essential instrument of God's life. God sums up the argument: "The problem is that people keep looking up, when they should look inside. . . . You want to see a miracle—then be a miracle."

Questions

• Why are human beings tempted to make God in our own image? What are the consequences?

• What is the grace that is offered to us through our interaction with the poor?

• What does this film have to say about looking for God "in all the wrong places"?

City of God

Starring Matheus Nachtergaele, Seu Jorge, and Alexandre Rodrigues.
Directed by Kátia Lund and Fernando Meirelles.
Rated R. 130 minutes. 2002. Portuguese with English subtitles.

Teachable moments: poverty, respect, social justice.

In the 1960s, to alleviate a housing crisis, the Brazilian government relocates the underclass to an area euphemistically called the City of God. By any name, it is a slum. Rocket is a boy born into poverty, but he exhibits a mature objectivity about it. He wants to be a photographer. Twenty years later, the town becomes a jungle of concrete high-rise apartments. The only thing recognizable is the poverty. The king of the 'hood is Li'l Zé, a drug baron and ruthless killer. Anyone threatening his power is instantly eliminated. Li'l Zé's touchstone is his childhood friend Bené. Rocket has grown up with these men and, using a stolen camera, he chronicles what he sees. Rocket wants to portray to the world the grim face of the City of God, but to do so he has to survive local civil wars and the incursion of drugged megalomaniacs wielding guns. What Rocket really wants is a chance to survive this hell.

To name this degrading place the City of God is both tragic and ironic. The name comes from chapter 21 of the Book of Revelation and refers to the city on the far side of Armageddon:

> I saw the holy city, the new Jerusalem, coming down out of heaven from God, prepared as a bride adorned for her husband. And I heard a loud voice from the throne saying,
> "See, the home of God is among mortals.
> He will dwell with them as their God;
> they will be his peoples,
> and God himself will be with them;
> he will wipe every tear from their eyes.
> Death will be no more;
> mourning and crying and pain will be no more."
>   (21:2–4)

Those destined for God's holy city will first survive the great persecution. These celestial citizens will witness the marrying of heaven and earth and gain eternal life.

Based on a true story, this arresting film portrays what it is to survive a great persecution. *City of God* is a war film. It is not pretty, describing a violent world in shocking detail. But it also underscores the realities of the cycle of poverty, the causes of crime, and the inheritance of disadvantage. The real cowards in this City of God are those who live outside it and let it happen, who allow generational poverty to take root. It condemns us for doing nothing locally and globally. We are our brothers' and sisters' keepers.

Nearly every aid agency speaks about the relationship between poverty and development, structural and social sin. Throwing money at an issue or area will not solve it. Long-lasting solutions require careful analysis of the causes of poverty, immediately attending to the need for safety and the essentials of life, and addressing the lack of dignity that deprivation bestows. A long-term commitment to education, health, and employment are vital. None of this is easy, especially when we prefer simple answers and quick fixes. *City of God* offers a ray of hope in the midst of social disintegration. The sign of hope is celebrated by a new name.

The actors in this film were amateurs, many of them from Rio's slums. Alexandre Rodrigues, who plays Rocket, lived in the City of God. Their performances are compelling, natural, and believable. They tell the rest of the world about their world. This film will give us pause when next we sing Dan Schutte's hymn, "Let us build the City of God, may our tears be turned into dancing. For Lord our light and our love, has turned the night into day."

Questions

• Where is God to be found in the City of God?

• What efforts are being made to address the underlying causes of poverty in our world today?

• How does our faith in Christ challenge us to be "our brother's keeper"?

Gallipoli

Starring Mel Gibson, Mark Lee, and Bill Hunter. Directed by Peter Weir.
Rated PG. 110 minutes. 1981.

Teachable moments: sacrificial love, martyrdom.

In 1914, Australia responds to Britain's request to help fight
World War I. Meanwhile, fresh-faced Archy Hamilton works on
his father's ranch in West Australia. His uncle is training him to
win the world championship in the 100-yard dash. On the track
at home, Archy already has it within his grasp.

Archy goes to town for an athletics carnival and is chased by
a recruiting officer. The idea of going overseas to fight for "God,
King, and Country" seems like a great adventure. Archy's sprint-
ing rival, Irish Catholic Frank Dunne, is not fond of the British
king or wars waged in his name. He resists the recruiting drive.

After Archy defeats Frank in the footrace, they hit the
road looking for work. Archy convinces Frank to join him in

volunteering for the army. With poor prospects at home, Frank relents. They eventually end up together in the 10th Regiment of the Light Horse Brigade, entirely composed of men from home. After halfhearted training in Egypt, they end up at Gallipoli, an escarpment on Turkey's west coast. Poorly planned, badly placed, outnumbered and outgunned, the Gallipoli campaign is a disaster. With poor communications between headquarters and trenches, runners are vital, and Archy is the quickest on the peninsula.

When 10th Light Horse is ordered to attack a Turkish stronghold, the men are petrified, especially Frank. Archy convinces his commanding officer, Major Barton, to let him replace Frank in the trench and make Frank the runner. As the hopeless battle is waged, the battalion is slaughtered. Despite all reason, Major Barton is ordered to proceed with the battle. The major appeals to General Gardner, and he calls for the charge to cease. Frank races back with the news, but arrives too late to save Archy.

Australia and New Zealand are distinctive in that their war memorial day, April 25, commemorates the beginning of a military disaster. In 1914, the population of Australia was 4.97 million. In World War I they lost 58,150 men, 8,709 killed in the first major commitment of troops at Gallipoli. Proportionally, it was even worse for New Zealand. The events that started at Gallipoli changed the history of both countries.

Given that it takes most of the film to get to the site of the battle, the movie is not primarily interested in the war. *Gallipoli* is primarily interested in heroic death. The allusions to death are everywhere in the film. Moses' sacrificial death in the desert is an atonement for sin that enables the Israelites to inherit the

Promised Land. In some schools of theology, Jesus is the definitive sacrifice offered in atonement for humanity's sins. Archy is a blood gift for God, King, and Country. When Archy takes Frank's place, he demonstrates the greatest Christian virtue: "No one has greater love than this, to lay down one's life for one's friends" (John 15:13).

Moses, Jesus, and Archy are faithful servants of a higher power, cut down before seeing the fruition of their work. All three pay the price for the sins of others. Their deaths are not meaningless, but a necessary requirement so that others may inherit a new identity, dignity, and perspective on their destiny. Their closest mates—respectively Joshua, Peter, and Frank—take up the story so that these martyrs become the measure by which all followers will be judged. Not just in wars are great battles fought. Being people for others means sometimes standing against society's values. Martyrdom comes in a variety of ways.

Questions

• In what sense does Archy suffer martyrdom?

• Is there a connection between the self-sacrifice of discipleship and giving one's life for one's country?

• What is meant by atonement of sins? How is it featured in the film?

Chariots of Fire

Starring Ben Cross, Ian Charleson, Ian Holm, John Gielgud, and Nigel Havers. Directed by Hugh Hudson. Rated PG. 123 minutes. 1981.

Teachable moments: conscience, Scripture, fundamentalism.

Before the 1924 Olympics, two runners emerge as Britain's favorites for the 100-meter race: missionary Eric Liddell and Harold Abrahams, the son of a Jewish migrant. Eric's heart is in the missions, but he sees his athletic prowess as a gift to be used for evangelization: "I believe God made me for a purpose, but he also made me fast."

Harold, enrolled at Cambridge, is desperate for acceptance among the British establishment and views sporting achievements as a springboard to commercial success. In the heats, Liddell beats Abrahams for a place in the final. The semifinal is scheduled for a Sunday. Liddell won't run because Sunday is the holy day of rest. Abrahams is chosen to run for England instead.

An aristocrat cedes his place in the 400-meter final, which is run on a Tuesday, to Liddell. Both men compete for Olympic glory.

Eric Liddell, as portrayed in this film, is a noble character. He obeys his conscience. The problem is: how well-informed was his conscience? Biblical fundamentalism is a social response to a complex world. Rather than live with ambiguity or complexity, fundamentalists sharply define the world in black and white. Liddell adheres to this perspective: "Compromise is the language of the devil." Liddell calls God a "divine dictator" whose laws are not to be disregarded. The interpretation of those laws is the real question.

Moses delivered the commandment about the Sabbath as a holy day of rest—the world's oldest labor law. It mirrored God's day off in the creation story. The sanctity of the Sabbath called for worship, but also the nonexploitation of human beings. The day in question was Saturday. *Sabbath* comes from the Hebrew word for "seventh." Strictly speaking, Sunday cannot be the seventh day. Jesus was raised from the dead on a Sunday, but there's no New Testament evidence that early Christians moved the Sabbath to a Sunday. Some evidence suggests they worshipped on two days—Saturday and Sunday. The Romans had an eight-day week, but with the rise of Christianity the Judeo-Christian seven-day week took effect, with Sunday as its first day.

St. Justin (c.100–c.165) was the first to record Sunday as the Christian holy day, and Tertullian (c.160–230) called Sunday "a day of rest." In 300 a church council made Sunday observance an absolute norm in the church. Sixteen centuries later, Eric Liddell won't run on Sunday because of what he thinks Scripture says.

Ironically for a biblical fundamentalist, Mr. Liddell unknowingly ends up defending tradition, not Scripture.

Biblical fundamentalism suffers from being ahistorical; the text has never been all there is. The Bible does not give us the Trinity as we understand it, nor the two natures of Christ as we define them, nor the role of the Holy Spirit, nor the precise books of Scripture itself—all these were determined by the church under the Spirit's guidance. Scripture and tradition remain equal resources of authority and inspiration.

Liddell's stand is decent, but his argument is flawed. Jesus insists, "The sabbath was made for humankind, and not humankind for the sabbath" (Mark 2:27). God is not a divine dictator. God is our faithful lover through every generation. I think God delights at us excelling in any way we can on any day of the week, especially if in the process we recognize the gift and the giver.

Questions

• How can the development of our natural gifts and talents be an expression of our faith in God?

• What challenges do you face today in keeping the Sabbath as a day of rest?

• What inherent stumbling blocks exist in biblical fundamentalism?

Tender Mercies

Starring Robert Duvall, Ellen Barkin, and Tess Harper. Directed by Bruce Beresford. Rated PG. 100 minutes. 1983.

Teachable moments: suffering, healing, baptism.

Mac Sledge was a star of the country-music circuit. He was also a champion drinker, and after years of hard living he disappeared. Finally sober, he winds up at a motel run by Rosa, a recent war widow and mother to Sonny. Mac does odd jobs around the place, falls in love with Rosa, and marries her. Word spreads that Mac Sledge has moved to town, and his fans come calling. Mac has to choose between his old life and the new one he has found with Rosa and Sonny. He must also be reconciled with his estranged daughter Sue Anne and ex-wife Dixie. In recognition of the healing that gradually takes place, Mac and Sonny get baptized.

Depression hangs like a pall over *Tender Mercies*—undiagnosed, untreated depression. Mac grieves for his lost life and dead daughter. Sue Anne grieves for the war hero who never came home. The public laments the star who faded away. Being lost hurts. *Tender Mercies* charts the wandering of lost souls. What makes this film inspiring is that it is also about the joy of being found. Mac finds sobriety and a wife. Sue Anne finds a husband. Sonny finds a father. The fans find Mac. Mac finds the way, the truth, and the life he wants.

First, however, painful lessons have to be learned from history. Finding a new page upon which to write involves reconciling the past. Reflecting on his history, Mac asks the pivotal question, "Why has God done this to me?" Why did God allow him to be an alcoholic and to lose his family? Why did God take Rosa's husband? For all believers, the meaning of suffering is the universal question.

The area of theology that wrestles with these "why" questions is called theodicy. How do we believe in a God of love when bad things happen to us? No answer is completely satisfying, least of all the idea that God sends bad events to teach us something. But a few things can be said about the reality of evil. God does not send evil. "God is light and in him there is no darkness at all" (1 John 1:5). Among God's teaching aids, death, disease, accidents, and natural disasters do not figure. If they did, then darkness would be in God.

This doesn't mean that we cannot learn from what we suffer. Indeed, with amazing grace, we do learn and grow beyond the question, "Why did God do this to me?" We may rightly wonder why God permits evil. But that is a very different matter than believing God directly wills tragedy into our lives.

One of the ways God cares for us when disaster strikes is through those around us. Mac, Sue Anne, and Sonny see in each other God's love and goodness in action. They are saved by the hands that caught them in the free fall of life. As they find each other, they find God, who never lost them in the first place.

Mac's baptism ritualizes his personal conversion, his sense of "becoming a new creation in Christ." He confronts his past in order to get closure on it. Mac learns to trust the Lord's tender mercies: "His tender mercies are over all His works" (Psalm 145:9 KJV). In the desert of our lives we often encounter God's mercies and must find the heart to welcome them in.

Questions

- Where does this film suggest that God's tender mercies may be found? Do you agree?

- What is the Christian response to the reality of evil in the world?

- How does the film depict the healing journey of being lost and found?

The Road Home

Starring Ziyi Zhang and Honglei Sun. Directed by Yimou Zhang. Rated G. 89 minutes. 1999. Mandarin with English subtitles.

Teachable moments: honoring parents, journey.

During a brutal winter, Luo Yusheng's father, Luo Changyu, dies. Now an urban businessman, Luo Yusheng returns to his village for the funeral. His mother, Zhao Di, and his teacher father lived in rural villages all their lives. Zhao Di insists her husband be buried in the village where they met. Luo Yusheng tries to explain that the family is not wealthy enough to pay pallbearers for a full day's trudging through the snow, but Zhao Di is unrelenting. Luo Yusheng reflects on his father's life of service. Meanwhile, word goes out that the teacher's body is to be brought home. Former students volunteer their services for the procession. Despite a blinding snowstorm, everyone turns out. Moved, the son fulfills his father's last wish—Luo Yusheng becomes a teacher, if only for a day, in the schoolroom where his father taught.

If ever there was a film on the fourth commandment, *The Road Home* is it. China's official atheism only proves the universality of the teaching. This gentle film explores why we honor our parents. Luo Yusheng wants to honor his father, but he is also practical. His mother knows the veneration with which her husband was held by his students. She gives them an opportunity to be generous.

The Road Home captures the respect with which teachers are held in China. Teaching is among one of the most revered professions in many Asian countries. Confucius taught that his disciples should "educate all without discrimination, and teach according to the abilities of one's students." Confucius saw the need to educate the whole person. He devised a syllabus of religion, music, archery, chariot driving, reading, writing, and mathematics. In the West, education is often seen as a commodity rather than a service. Consequently, teachers are accorded less respect. They "do their job"—delivering value for the educational dollar. Nonetheless, many dedicated teachers inspire their students with the priceless gift of education.

Luo Yusheng fails to appreciate how the students share the affection and respect he holds for his father. Being a father for others takes many forms, but the honor accorded the role is universal. The commandment to honor a parent was not unique to Israel; nearly every law code of ancient civilizations contained a similar requirement. The fourth commandment is the first one in the Decalogue to move beyond our duty toward God, and it comes before all other obligations to society.

Some people find it hard to honor their fathers or mothers today. We cannot cloak in sentiment criminal neglect or the harm done to some children by their parents. Parents receive honor from their children because they earn it. In modern parlance, then, the commandment is about mutual obligation. Zhao Di knows the villagers loved her husband like a father, so even though her request is outrageous, she knows they will honor it.

The Road Home shows the importance of farewell rituals. The coffin is bound in a special cloth. We place a pall over the coffin to recall the white robe of baptism. Symbols of the teacher's life are held, and these evoke stories about him. We display mementoes of the deceased, which trigger memories and eulogies. They have a procession for the mourners. So do we. Meals play a central role in remembering Luo Changyu. We have the Eucharist. Finally, travel is central to the story. As Luo Yusheng comprehends, "The road is part of their love story." May our journey be part of the Christian love story.

Questions

• How is education perceived in Western culture today? What implications might that have for religious education?

• How does the fourth commandment lead Christians beyond a superficial respect for parents?

• What is the importance of ritual for expressing our deepest feelings?

The Magdalene Sisters

Starring Geraldine McEwan, Anne-Marie Duff, Nora-Jane Noone, Dorothy Duffy, and Eileen Walsh. Written and directed by Peter Mullan. Rated R. 119 minutes. 2002.

Teachable moments: sexual abuse, original goodness.

In nineteenth-century Ireland, little distinction was made between church and state. Religious communities ran institutions on behalf of the government. One civic concern was unmarried mothers, often called "Magdalenes." Nuns founded institutions known as Magdalene laundries to which these women were committed. They also took in wayward girls, "temptresses," and girls who had been raped. They were effective prisons within which women worked without recompense and were treated harshly. Here we meet Crispina and Rose, who are unwed mothers. We also meet

Margaret who is raped by a cousin and committed to the laundry by the parish priest. A beautiful girl, Bernadette, is locked up "for her own good" as a threat to her own and boys' virtue. At the hands of repressive nuns, these women endure physical and sexual abuse and tragic deprivation. Three survive to tell their stories.

The events are telescoped, compressed in time and place, but all the stories are purported to be true. No one who has followed the scandals of sexual and physical abuse in recent years can doubt the portrayals. What telescoping does, however, is to eliminate almost all elements of humanity from the institution. The laundry is a concentration camp. Not one of the nuns is remotely kind. The girls have temporary alliances rather than friendships. The priest is an abuser. The superior is a sociopath. The culpability of families and the state is viewed in only a limited way. Yet this film remains important to all of us.

Reprehensibly, some in need have come to church institutions over the years only to be harmed. The church, meant to set the standard of morality, care, and safety, must practice what it preaches. In 2000, Pope John Paul II called for a "purification of memory." This purification aimed at a full disclosure of past abuses as the only route to reconciling with the victims because "the consequences of the past still make themselves felt and can persist as tensions in the present. The purification of memory is thus 'an act of courage and humility in recognizing the wrongs done by those who have borne or bear the name of Christian'" (CDF: *Memory and Reconciliation*: introduction: 1999). *The Magdalene Sisters* helps in this purification because it does not allow the community to ignore the experiences some have had in the church's care. Repentance must start with the truth no matter how painful it is to say or hear it; some have been damaged for life at the hands of those in whose company they should have been safe.

Two issues warrant examination. The heresy of Jansenism marked the Irish Catholic Church. Jansenism holds that we are born bad. Only through a strict moral life can we hope to be saved. It views sexual desire and activity as the worst sins, from which it is difficult to obtain God's forgiveness. This film demonstrates the institutionalization of Jansenism. In a worldview preoccupied with "sins of the flesh," it is acceptable to save young women—not to mention their seemingly uncontrollable male partners—by locking these women up and working them to exhaustion.

Everyone in this scenario is a victim to some degree: the women, scapegoated by their families; the nuns who believed they acted rightly (some coming from the ranks of the laundry's inmates); and the community, infected with bad theology. Borrowing from George Orwell, we might say that under Jansenism, all are victims, but some are more victimized than others. What we do about the most victimized in our community determines who we are.

Questions

• What are the responsibilities of the families who sent their daughters into the Magdalene system?

• Why is it important to keep before us the abuses suffered in the name of religion?

• How effective are public apologies issued by religious and political leaders in healing the effects of past social sins?

The Passion of
the Christ

Starring James Caviezel and Monica Bellucci. Directed by Mel Gibson.
Rated R. 127 minutes. 2004.

Teachable moments: Passion, gospel, suffering.

No one can doubt the personal devotion and faith Mel Gibson brought to this film. He put his money where his soul is, and this investment has paid off. Gibson stands in a long line of such distinguished directors as Cecil B. DeMille, George Stevens, Martin Scorsese, and Pier Paolo Pasolini, who brought their particular passions to bear on that of Jesus. My major concern about *The Passion of the Christ* is that Mel Gibson went around the world telling viewers that his film "is the most historically accurate film ever made about the Passion." More on that in a moment.

Most portrayals of Jesus provide some insight into the historical events recorded in the Gospels. But every Passion play, and that's the genre of these films, is also a commentary on the here and now. During the roaring twenties, *The King of Kings* gave the world an epic and spectacular Jesus. In the 1960s, *The Greatest Story Ever Told* bombed at the box office because it brought nothing fresh to the story. Pasolini's *The Gospel According to St. Matthew* has more to do with Marx than Matthew, and by the 1980s *The Last Temptation of Christ* had Jesus dream about what life would be like with a wife and kids.

One of the problems with Gibson's *Passion* is that, like most Jesus films, it treats the four Gospels as a smorgasbord and takes what it likes from each. This follows in the devotional tradition of the stations of the cross, but makes it wrong to sell the film to the public as "historically accurate." The Gospels are four highly stylized, inspired portraits of Jesus' life, death, and resurrection. The differences are especially evident when they turn to the passion of Jesus. In Mark, Jesus suffers grievously and feels abandoned on the cross. Matthew sees Jesus as the rejected messiah of Israel and is noted for its anti-Jewish tone. Luke has Jesus reach out to gentiles and sinners, even on the cross. John's Jesus is poised, controlled, and majestic as he enters into his suffering and death.

The liturgical life of the church respects these distinctions. We never liberally jump between these narratives. The process of biblical smorgasbord does a disservice to the integrity of each text. Adding to the problem of historical accuracy in *The Passion* is the use of extraneous material inflicted on the homogenized narrative.

Gibson claims one of the texts that affected him most deeply in his preparation was *The Dolorous Passion of Our Lord Jesus Christ*, written by German mystic Anne Catherine Emmerich and published in 1833. This book records her private revelations about the death of Jesus. Unfortunately, Gibson incorporates a number of scenes from this book into his film: a confrontation after the arrest between a chained Jesus and Judas, a much larger role for Pilate's wife, a tender meeting between Jesus and his mother, a raven picking out the eyes of the bad thief, and a waterfall of blood pouring over the Roman centurion as he pierces Jesus' side. Anne Catherine Emmerich's recent beatification may obscure the fact that her case languished for years until her writings were excluded from her cause.

Beyond its use of sources, the film is worrying for its graphic violence, which is obscenely brutal. The church rightly condemns other films for using graphic violence. Some Christians argue that we need to be shocked into understanding how Jesus suffered and died for us. Shock is a questionable tool for conversion. Once we accept this premise, the question arises, "Was *The Passion* violent enough? Should future films about Jesus' death be even more violent so an even greater number of people might be shocked into knowing Christ's love?" Is graphic violence acceptable in films about forgiveness and sacrificial love? If so, we might have to endorse brutal portrayals of gang rapes, capital punishments, and genocides as long as they come to a redemptive conclusion.

In *The Passion of the Christ*, Jesus is portrayed as a masochist, as not just accepting the sufferings that came his way but looking for more. What made the death of Jesus unique was not his physical suffering but the submission of his spirit. That's why the New Testament does not overly dwell on the physical details of the Passion. Others have died cruel deaths, but no one, we believe, carried what Jesus did as he suffered and died.

The third troublesome issue in this film is its alleged anti-Semitism. I do not think Christians are in the best position to make this call. It would be akin to straight people telling homosexual people about homophobia, men telling women about sexism, and white people telling black people what is and is not racist. It is up to Jewish people to say how they experienced the film, and they seem divided on the question. We can see why some think it is anti-Semitic. There are stereotypically gratuitous portraits of "the Jews," especially in the scenes involving Judas and the betrayal money. Worst of all is the exaggerated role given to Caiaphas, the chief priest. The real baddies in the film are Caiaphas and the councilors who lead the Jewish crowd to bay for Jesus' blood. The quote from Matthew 27—"His blood be on us and on our children" (27:25)—is the only line in Aramaic not given an English subtitle. Equally disturbing is the personification of Satan as a ghostly woman nursing a disabled child, wandering through the Jewish crowd pleased at her handiwork. Theologically we believe we all carry responsibility for the death of Jesus.

The Passion of the Christ is, in moments, a moving portrait, but it's also a highly evangelical work. The title says it all. This film is not interested in the passion of the historical Jesus but the passion of "the Christ," the only Son of God. This is key to its meaning.

The presentations of Jesus' passion that touch me most deeply are the ones told in the context of the whole of Jesus' life and ministry. These films have a less hectoring tone, are more faithful to Gospel sources, and show us, for longer than one resuscitating minute at the end, that Jesus' resurrection demonstrates why God had the last word on his Son's faithful and self-sacrificing love for us, and how his love leads all people everywhere to know that they have the hope of eternal life.

Questions

- Did the brutal images of Jesus suffering and dying inspire you to live your life differently?

- Since many people die cruel and violent deaths, what makes Jesus' death redemptive?

Appendix 1:
Movies by MPAA Rating

G: General Audiences. All ages admitted.

Babette's Feast, 22

Finding Nemo, 126

A Man for All Seasons, 7

The Road Home, 144

PG: Parental Guidance Suggested. Some material may not be suitable for children.

Chariots of Fire, 138

Dead Poets Society, 31

Gallipoli, 135

Gandhi, 28

Groundhog Day, 1

The Mission, 4

Places in the Heart, 13

Shadowlands, 46

Tender Mercies, 141

The Truman Show, 74

PG-13: Parents Strongly Cautioned. Some material may be inappropriate for children under 13.

The Apostle, 71

Bruce Almighty, 129

Chocolat, 92

Hannah and Her Sisters, 19

In America, 105

Life is Beautiful, 61

The Lord of the Rings Trilogy:

   The Fellowship of the Rings

   The Two Towers

   The Return of the King, 94

Philadelphia, 49

Romero, 34

Whale Rider, 117

R: Restricted. Under 17 requires accompanying parent or adult guardian.

Billy Elliott, 83

Bowling for Columbine, 102

City of God, 132

The Crime of Father Amaro, 123

Dead Man Walking, 58

Erin Brockovich, 86

The Exorcist, 80

Gladiator, 89

Glory, 99

The Godfather; The Godfather Part II, 64

The Hurricane, 120

The Insider, 77

Italian for Beginners, 114

JFK, 37

The Magdalene Sisters, 147

Appendix 2:
Movie Licensing Information

The U.S. Copyright Law of 1976 requires a license for showing commercial videos at church events. Movie videos are released "For Home Use Only," and it is illegal to show them in other settings.

However, you can get an umbrella license from the Motion Picture Licensing Corporation (MPLC) (1-800-462-8855 or www.mplc.com) who may refer you to Christian Video Licensing International (www.CVLI.org). The licensing period is generally one year, and there is a low annual fee based on the size of the congregation. You can be licensed over the phone by the MPLC to start showing videos immediately, and the MPLC will bill the church and send information regarding the stipulations of the license. You might check with your diocesan office or denominational headquarters, since they may have worked out discount licensing rates with CVLI.

The license covers films from nearly fifty studios. A list will be provided to you when you apply for your umbrella license. Studios are continually being added to the list; a studio not on the list now may be added later. (If a studio that owns the copyright of a film you want to show at church is not on the list, you must write directly to the producers for permission.) Before using them, you should check the current list for the status of the movies in this book.

If you don't want to go the licensing route, the alternative is to ask group members to watch a video at home and discuss it at a subsequent gathering.

More information on legal issues is readily available at either Web site.

From Barbara Mraz, *Finding Faith at the Movies*, (New York: Morehouse Publishing, 2004), 3–4.

Bibliography

Babington, Bruce, and Peter W. Evans. *Biblical Epics: Sacred Narrative in the Hollywood Cinema*. Manchester: Manchester University Press, 1993.

Bergesen, Albert J., and Andrew M. Greely. *God in the Movies*. New Brunswick, NJ: Transaction, 2000.

Blake, Richard A. *Afterimage: The Indelible Catholic Imagination of Six American Filmmakers*. Chicago: Loyola Press, 2000.

De Bleeckere, Sylvain. "The Religious Dimension of Cinematic Consciousness." In *New Image of Religious Film*, edited by John R. May. Kansas City, MO: Sheed & Ward, 1997.

Fraser, Peter. *Images of the Passion: The Sacramental Mode in Film*. Westpoint, CT: Praeger, 1998.

Graham, David John. "The Uses of Film in Theology." In *Explorations in Theology and Film: Movies and Meaning*, edited by Clive Marsh and Gaye Ortiz. Malden, MA: Blackwell, 1997.

Gunning, Tom. "An Aesthetic of Astonishment: Early Film and the (In) Credulous Spectator." *Art & Text* 34 (Spring 1989): 31–45.

Holloway, Ronald. *Beyond the Image: Approaches to the Religious Dimension in the Cinema*. Geneva: World Council of Churches in Cooperation with Interfilm, 1977.

Hurley, Neil P. *Theology through Film*. New York: Harper & Row, 1970.

Jewett, Robert. *Saint Paul at the Movies: The Apostle's Dialogue with American Culture*. Louisville, KY: Westminster/John Knox Press, 1993.

John Paul II. "A Communicator of Culture and Values," World Communications Day Message, Vatican City, May 25, 1995, *Acta Apostolica Sedis*, LXXXVII: 197.

————. "Address to the Academy of Motion Picture Arts and Sciences," Los Angeles, September 15, 1987, *Acta Apostolica Sedis*, LXXXIX: 781–87.

————. "Proclaiming Christ at the Dawn of the New Millennium," World Communications Day Message, Vatican City, June 4, 2000, *Acta Apostolica Sedis*, XCII: 234.

Johnston, Robert K. *Reel Spirituality: Theology and Film in Dialogue*. Grand Rapids, MI: Baker Books, 2000.

Jones, G. William. *Sunday Night at the Movies*. Richmond, VA: John Knox Press, 1967.

Marsh, Clive and Gaye Ortiz. *Explorations in Theology and Film*. Malden, MA: Blackwell, 1997.

Martin, Joel W., and Conrad E. Ostwalt Jr. *Screening the Sacred: Religion, Myth, and Ideology in American Popular Film*. Boulder, CO: Westview Press, 1995.

May, John R. *New Image of Religious Film*. Kansas City, MO: Sheed & Ward, 1997.

May, John R., and Michael Bird. *Religion in Film*. Knoxville, TN: University of Tennessee Press, 1982.

Medved, Michael. *Hollywood vs. America: Popular Culture and the War on Traditional Values*. New York: HarperCollins, 1992.

Miles, Margaret R. *Seeing and Believing: Religion and Values in the Movies.* Boston: Beacon Press, 1996.

Schrader, Paul. *Transcendental Style in Film: Ozu, Bresson, Dreyer.* New York: Da Capo Press, 1988.

Stone, Bryan P. *Faith and Film: Theological Themes at the Cinema.* St. Louis, MO: Chalice Press, 2000.

Wollen, Peter. *Signs and Meaning in the Cinema.* Bloomington, IN: Indiana University Press, 1972.

About the Author

Richard Leonard, SJ, is a Jesuit of the Australian Province. He is the director of the Australian Catholic Film Office, a consultant to the Australian Catholic Bishop's Media Committee, and a film critic for all the major Catholic newspapers of Australia.

He combines his film scholarship with an active writing and lecturing career in the areas of cinema, culture, and religion. He has lectured across Australia and in England, Ireland, Scotland, Italy, Pakistan, India, and the United States, and has a master's degree in systematic theology and a doctorate in cinema studies.

Index of Movies

Index of Teachable Moments

Index of Release Dates